Cambridge Elements

Elements in Critical Issues in Teacher Education
edited by
Tony Loughland
University of New South Wales
Andy Gao
University of New South Wales
Hoa T. M. Nguyen
University of New South Wales

ONLINE TEACHER EDUCATION AND INTERACTIVE TECHNOLOGIES

Seyum Getenet
University of Southern Queensland
Eseta Tualaulelei
University of Southern Queensland

Shaftesbury Road, Cambridge CB2 8EA, United Kingdom

One Liberty Plaza, 20th Floor, New York, NY 10006, USA

477 Williamstown Road, Port Melbourne, VIC 3207, Australia

314–321, 3rd Floor, Plot 3, Splendor Forum, Jasola District Centre, New Delhi – 110025, India

103 Penang Road, #05–06/07, Visioncrest Commercial, Singapore 238467

Cambridge University Press is part of Cambridge University Press & Assessment, a department of the University of Cambridge.

We share the University's mission to contribute to society through the pursuit of education, learning and research at the highest international levels of excellence.

www.cambridge.org
Information on this title: www.cambridge.org/9781009527309

DOI: 10.1017/9781009527354

© Seyum Getenet and Eseta Tualaulelei 2026

This publication is in copyright. Subject to statutory exception and to the provisions of relevant collective licensing agreements, no reproduction of any part may take place without the written permission of Cambridge University Press & Assessment.

When citing this work, please include a reference to the DOI 10.1017/9781009527354

First published 2026

A catalogue record for this publication is available from the British Library

ISBN 978-1-009-52730-9 Hardback
ISBN 978-1-009-52731-6 Paperback
ISSN 2755-1202 (online)
ISSN 2755-1199 (print)

Cambridge University Press & Assessment has no responsibility for the persistence or accuracy of URLs for external or third-party internet websites referred to in this publication and does not guarantee that any content on such websites is, or will remain, accurate or appropriate.

For EU product safety concerns, contact us at Calle de José Abascal, 56, 1°, 28003 Madrid, Spain, or email eugpsr@cambridge.org

Online Teacher Education and Interactive Technologies

Elements in Critical Issues in Teacher Education

DOI: 10.1017/9781009527354
First published online: January 2026

Seyum Getenet
University of Southern Queensland

Eseta Tualaulelei
University of Southern Queensland

Author for correspondence: Seyum Getenet, Seyum.Getenet@unisq.edu.au

Abstract: This Element focuses on the role of interactive technologies in enhancing pre-service teachers' engagement with learning in online environments. It begins with a brief overview of the current state of teacher education, focusing on online teaching. This is followed by analysing the concept of engagement, underscoring its importance for pre-service teachers studying online. The Element then explores various dimensions of engagement – cognitive, behavioural, affective, and other – and how interactive technologies can enhance these dimensions in online learning. A key feature of this Element is its exploration of key challenges that teacher educators and pre-service teachers encounter when using interactive technologies with practical recommendations for addressing them. The concluding section shifts the focus to the future, offering recommendations for how teacher education can use interactive technologies to 'grow' teacher educators who can engage their students. Throughout the Element, practical examples complement theoretical discussions to bridge the gap between theory and practice.

This Element also has a video abstract:
www.cambridge.org/*EITE_Getenet_abstract*

Keywords: teacher education, online learning, learning engagement, digital technologies, pre-service teachers

© Seyum Getenet and Eseta Tualaulelei 2026

ISBNs: 9781009527309 (HB), 9781009527316 (PB), 9781009527354 (OC)
ISSNs: 2755-1202 (online), 2755-1199 (print)

Contents

1 Introduction   1

2 Cognitive Engagement   13

3 Behavioural Engagement   21

4 Affective Engagement   28

5 Other Types of Engagement   40

6 Where to from Here?   49

References   60

1 Introduction

Online teacher education is expanding. Even before the COVID-19 pandemic forced initial teacher education online, almost half of Australia's initial teacher education providers offered online and blended learning options (Dyment & Downing, 2019). Wood (2022) noted that the pandemic accelerated the upward trend in online education and forecast the upward trend to continue. In a literature review about online teaching and learning practices in teacher education, Carrillo and Flores (2020, p. 478) identified the need for 'a comprehensive and solid view of the pedagogy of online education'. They recognised that teacher education appears to have been swept along with the broader expansion of online education, and that insufficient attention has been given to *online* teacher education. How does it promote the qualities that a 'good teacher' should have? How can teacher educators deliver teacher education online in ways that achieve the goals of the teaching profession? How can we keep pre-service teachers engaged in online learning? These questions and more are addressed in this Element, which aims both to contribute to much-needed discussion about the nature of online teacher education and to highlight the role of interactive technologies in engaging pre-service teachers.

Pre-service teachers were traditionally taught face-to-face. The education profession values teachers' face-to-face interactions and rapport-building with both students and colleagues, and the public also regards as 'good teachers' those who have positive relationships with their students (Haas et al., 2023). Face-to-face classes enabled teacher educators to build rapport with students and encourage them to build rapport with each other through classroom interactions, group work, discussions, and the like. It also enabled them to model quality teaching practices, attend to students' learning needs in real time, and capitalise on the benefits of having everyone focused on the same ideas, issues, or challenges at the same time. Yet, face-to-face classes were hampered by their fixed location in space and time. Rural, regional, and remote students lacked the opportunity to participate without incurring significant financial and personal costs. Moreover, delivery at fixed times made attendance difficult for those who had clashes with work, family, or other commitments. Face-to-face classes were also more expensive for educational institutions which paid the same amount for real estate, overheads, and other expenses whether a class had 300 students or 10. To solve the issues of fixed location, fixed time, and expense, universities have turned to technology.

The rise of online education can be traced back several decades. While education at a distance or by correspondence has a long history, it was not until personal computers became available and affordable to the public in the 1980s that online education became feasible (Harasim, 2000; Morabito, 1999). In the early part of this century, Taylor (2001) foresaw that online education 'has the potential to deliver a quantum leap in economies of scale and associated cost-effectiveness' (p. 4), and this became one of the driving factors for universities to integrate more and more online components into their offerings. Another driving factor was the rapid advances in technology. The Internet has become more widespread and accessible, developing from dial-up to broadband and now to wireless services covering a broad geographical range. In addition, the types of advanced personal devices that people could use to access the Internet expanded – laptops, tablets, smartphones, smart televisions, and so on – and they became more affordable. These developments helped online learning become more widely accepted and so, for the past two decades, teacher education has been delivered online across the world (Burns, 2023; Hurlbut, 2018). In Australia, where we are writing, the first teachers who studied online or blended programmes graduated in the early 2000s (Downing et al., 2019) and nowadays, teacher graduates are more likely than not to have studied online for some part of their degrees.

Parallel to these developments in the delivery of teacher education, the teaching profession itself was changing. The gradual creep of neoliberal values into education was a concern for many before the turn of the century (Apple, 1995; Bostock, 1999; Bourdieu, 1998; Bourdieu & Passeron, 1990; Noble, 1998), but subsequently, these concerns became a reality. Globalisation catalysed the standardisation of educational goals and curricula worldwide, with many countries reforming their educational systems to introduce frameworks and standards for school and teacher quality. Further, modern technology rapidly disseminated ideas and enabled the collection of large-scale and detailed data, ranking and comparing students, schools, and school systems (Chong, 2018; Lingard, 2018). Teachers are now subjected to more scrutiny than ever before in the name of teacher quality and public accountability.

Not only has the nature of teacher education changed, but so have the students. The extensive reach of the Internet and university equity commitments to widening participation have resulted in a more diverse body of students becoming pre-service teachers. Although still a largely feminised profession, pre-service teachers come from a wider range of socio-economic, cultural and linguistic backgrounds, and life stages (Stone et al., 2019). In addition, some studies have identified a difference between generations. Millennials – those born after 1980 – are said to have different expectations of initial teacher education than previous generations. Millennials may be more tech-savvy, socially and environmentally conscious, and self-focused compared with other generations (Castro, 2010; Donnison, 2009; Mäkinen et al., 2018). At the same time, one study has shown that millennials are less concerned with assessment and are not confident in critiquing and giving feedback to others (Clark & Byrnes, 2015). Similarly, Generation Z learners, born between 1997 and 2012, were born into life with digital technology and can multitask with multiple applications open on one device and multiple devices operating simultaneously (Schnackenberg, 2019). This generation, however, reportedly needs more guidance with critical analysis and creatively applying knowledge. If initial teacher education is to be responsive to the diversity of backgrounds and experiences of today's pre-service teachers, then more knowledge is needed about how best to engage them online.

Another consideration is that the days of sterile online education, where learners accessed static resources and engaged in individual learning, are well behind us in today's multimodal world. Learners are immersed in technology daily and they expect their online learning experiences to be modern and dynamic. With virtual reality, for example, teachers can experience classroom environments before setting foot in a school. This has value for building up pre-service teachers' confidence to lead a class and it helps them develop a sense of teaching presence (Australian Institute for Teaching and School Leadership, 2023b). The contemporary pre-service teacher who is studying online expects to learn with and about technology beyond discussion forums and multimedia that does not require more than page turning or scrolling. Teacher educators must make an effort to create online professional learning communities that promote a sense of belonging for students who may never meet in person but can be considered online colleagues. These developments warrant a closer examination of online teacher education as a phenomenon, particularly in terms of how it promotes the dispositions and understandings that are valued by the teaching profession.

The role of teacher educators in facilitating these online learning experiences is important. Most teacher educators design their own courses either alone, with a teaching team, or with the support of an educational designer (a role ideally expert in the technological aspects of online course delivery). This means that the technology used in a course is strongly influenced by the teacher educators' self-efficacy for using technology for teaching. However, time and resource pressures mean that teacher educators do not always have the capacity or disposition to learn about new technologies or innovate with them for teaching (Burke et al., 2022; Gregory & Lodge, 2015; Watty et al., 2016). Universities may invest large amounts of money into advanced technologies, but their uptake largely rests with teaching faculty.

As teachers in initial teacher education, we have written this Element for the teaching academic who wants to engage their pre-service teachers who are studying online. We understand teaching to be a relational profession, predicated on the human and social interactions that occur between teachers and learners as well as among learners. We teach mathematics education at the primary level (Seyum) and literacy and intercultural communication for the early years (Eseta). We believe that online education has been beneficial for initial teacher education, but having taught face-to-face for as many years as we have online, we are also cognisant of the limitations of the online learning environment. The following section discusses student engagement to address some of these limitations.

1.1 The What and Why of 'Student Engagement' for Online Study

Online students typically experience less success with their studies. They have poorer retention and completion rates than on campus cohorts (Bawa, 2016; Stone et al., 2019), and online pre-service teachers are no different. The Australian Institute of Teaching and School Leadership [AITSL] (2018) followed up six years after pre-service teachers had started to study for an initial teacher education qualification. They found that 'only 50 per cent of off campus students completed their ITE program compared with 66 per cent of on campus and 68 per cent of mixed attendance students' (p. 15). AITSL did not attribute these figures to the mode of learning. In other words, studying online was not, per se, to blame for student attrition. Instead, AITSL attributed student attrition to life-stage factors such as '"family responsibilities", "paid work responsibilities", "workload difficulties", and "study/life balance"' (p. 15). Contemporary students who choose to study online are usually more mature, studying part-time, with financial and familial commitments that those who study face-to-face may not have. Therefore, it has been necessary to examine how to retain online pre-service teachers. While we could explore the choice of technologies, course design and faculty characteristics and skills – all known to influence online student success (Dacko et al., 2015; Ellis & Bliuc, 2019) – it is ultimately students who choose how they will engage and participate in online study. For this reason, 'student engagement' has become a focus for understanding whether students are likely to succeed with online study. Although we will discuss online student engagement shortly, we will first look at the origins of the concept.

Online student engagement has its roots in studies of student engagement in traditional educational settings which proposed engagement as a construct that fused together the individual and contextual factors contributing to students' education experiences and success (e.g., Fredricks et al., 2004; Krause & Coates, 2008; Kuh, 2003). These studies and others promoted engagement as constructed of multiple interrelated and overlapping dimensions. For example, in the seminal study by Fredricks et al. (2004, p. 60), behavioural, emotional, and cognitive engagements were described as such:

Behavioral engagement draws on the idea of participation; it includes involvement in academic and social or extracurricular activities and is considered crucial for achieving positive academic outcomes and preventing dropping out. *Emotional engagement* encompasses positive and negative reactions to teachers, classmates, academics, and school and is presumed to create ties to an institution and influence willingness to do the work. Finally, *cognitive engagement* draws on the idea of investment; it incorporates thoughtfulness and willingness to exert the effort necessary to comprehend complex ideas and master difficult skills.

These dimensions are malleable so they can potentially be addressed separately and together. Historical studies of engagement were focused on students in compulsory school settings. However, the issue of engagement has recently come to the fore in higher education where the number of online students has steadily increased while their retention and completion rates have remained significantly lower compared with on-campus cohorts (Bawa, 2016; Muljana & Luo, 2019; Stone et al., 2019). This has expanded the application of student engagement and prompted research into how to better engage online students.

As education has moved more into online settings, the notion of student engagement has evolved. There is no consensus on a definition of online student engagement, but at its core, it describes the various ways that students engage and connect with online learning resources and educational institutions (Bedenlier et al., 2020; Kahu, 2011; Kahu & Nelson, 2017; Tualaulelei et al., 2021). Student engagement may not matter so much in intensive block courses (Goode et al., 2022). However, it is widely considered essential for regular length (semester or trimester) courses because it helps student retention and academic achievement. Past ideas about online student engagement emphasised students' commitment and efforts towards their studies but these definitions – mostly focused on behavioural engagement – may not sufficiently represent how particular groups of students engage (Dixson, 2015; Stone & O'Shea, 2019; Tualaulelei et al., 2021). Contemporary cohorts of pre-service teachers are often studying online for the first time, as complete novices to higher education, or having last studied at university before the advent of online education. They may not be prepared for the isolation, self-driven learning, and asynchronous communication that are characteristic of online study. They may be unsure of *how* to engage online.

Some definitions continue to place the onus on the student as responsible for online student engagement (for example, Dixson, 2015), while others have expanded and refined the traditional notion. For example, Garrison (2017) created the widely used 'community of inquiry' framework conceptualising the educational experience as including social, cognitive, and *teaching* presence and three dimensions of engagement: engagement with participants, engagement with content, and engagement with goals or direction. Similarly, Redmond et al. (2018) characterised online student engagement as having five dimensions – cognitive, behavioural, emotional, collaborative, and social. The addition of social and collaborative dimensions to the dimensions established by Fredricks et al. (2004) acknowledges the importance of these connections for online learners who usually experience isolation and a feeling of disconnection from their online peers and the institution they are studying with. These expanded definitions further recognise that engagement is not merely the responsibility of students, but also that of educators and higher education institutions.

As teacher educators, we consider the idea of online student engagement to be essential to modern teaching and learning. If we can understand the ways that students engage online, we can design courses that better address these types of engagement. If we can understand more about why online pre-service teachers disengage, we can proactively address issues within our influence. There is much potential for online student engagement to promote improved learning outcomes for online pre-service teachers and more focused ways of engaging to ensure that both faculty and student time is put to good use. The next section presents our ideas in relation to what we have termed 'interactive technologies'.

1.2 What Are 'Interactive Technologies'?

'Interactive technologies' are online and virtual tools that allow students to communicate and learn synchronously or asynchronously (Getenet & Tualaulelei, 2023; Pifarre, 2019). With technology, the term 'interactive' means that information flows from the technology to the user and vice versa, and that the technology is responsive to the user's input (Oxford University Press, 2025). In other words, interactive technologies require action or communication from the user to which the technology reciprocates with a response. They differ from other information or media technologies like static documents or videos because interactive technologies require students to actively engage, manipulate, or interact with them. Examples of interactive technologies include Kahoot! (Dianati et al., 2020; Licorish et al., 2018), Padlet (Dianati et al., 2020; Ellis, 2015), Google Docs (Neumann & Kopcha, 2019; Suwantarathip & Wichadee, 2014), and quizzes (Jones et al., 2021), to name a few.

The notion of interactivity also extends to the platforms and pedagogies within which the technologies are used. Some learning management systems are created with pedagogical approaches in mind. Moodle, for example, proceeds from a social constructionist perspective that values collaboration, creation, observation and participation, transformation and flexibility (Dougiamas, 2025), so the platform is set up for educators who value this same approach to teaching and learning. However, in the hands of a didactic educator, Moodle may merely be used as a repository of resources that learners need to access and learn from on their own. Interactive technologies, therefore, rely on pedagogies that encourage participatory and active learning, group collaboration, and student agency. They also offer benefits for teaching. Interactive technologies can improve pedagogical practices through increasing efficiency and communication in learning activities (Dunn & Kennedy, 2019). Interactive technologies have also been shown to enhance assessment and feedback practices (Deeley, 2018), and they are seen as responsive and accommodating to diverse students' learning needs (Sugden et al., 2021). When used purposefully, these technologies can promote creativity (Pifarre, 2019).

There are, of course, several emerging technologies that are also interactive such as virtual worlds like *Second Life*, social media, augmented or virtual reality, artificial intelligence (standalone or integrated with other technologies), and educational (or 'serious') games. However, many of these have not yet fulfilled their potential for education as much as expected. Most of these technologies in higher education have not been widely adopted due to high costs, limited accessibility, or a lack of knowledge among teacher educators. In addition, research tends to focus on exploring these technologies for content delivery rather than for the development of higher-order cognitive skills. Therefore, we leave these technologies for others to explore. In this Element, we focus on those interactive technologies that any teacher educator or pre-service teacher with the Internet can access, have low barriers to access and use (not much training is needed to get started), and can serve clear educational goals.

Another point to note is that this Element is not addressing pre-service teachers learning about interactive technologies or Information Communications Technology (ICT) as a content focus. Neither is it about how to use interactive technologies for curriculum and lesson planning or for K-12 classroom instruction. This Element is written for teacher educators who teach online and who want to know more about how interactive technologies can engage their pre-service teachers who are studying online.

1.3 Our Research

This Element is based on our research, carried out over the past several years, about online student engagement, the details of which can be found in various publications (Getenet & Tualaulelei, 2023; Getenet et al., 2022; Singh et al., 2023; Tualaulelei, 2020; Tualaulelei et al., 2021). These studies used the pragmatic approaches of action research and design-based research, which are appropriate for initiatives aimed at improving educational practices and understandings, and which were selected for their capacity to create adaptive solutions for practical problems, their utility for shorter-term projects, and their suitability for projects exploring technological interventions (Anderson & Shattuck, 2012; McKay & Marshall, 2001; Mills, 2007; Pool & Laubscher, 2016; Zheng, 2015).

The studies were carried out through online courses we facilitated at a School of Education at a regional university in Australia. All four courses are part of initial teacher education degrees, namely:

- a fourth-year primary education undergraduate mathematics course in the Bachelor of Education (Primary) with 74 students,
- a fourth-year primary education undergraduate mathematics course in the Bachelor of Education (Primary) with 90 students,
- a first-year early childhood education literacy course in the Bachelor of Early Education with 21 students, and
- a first-year early childhood and primary postgraduate literacy course in the Masters of Learning and Teaching (Early Childhood) with 126 students.

The mathematics courses provided pre-service teachers with pedagogical and content knowledge for teaching mathematics in the primary school context, while the literacy and intercultural education courses developed pre-service teachers' knowledge for teaching these areas to children aged from birth to 8 years of age, either in pre-school or in school settings. Each course had ten modules of weekly content, including a two-hour synchronous tutorial using Zoom (zoom.us), an application that provides audio and video, breakout rooms, online chat, sharing functions, and teaching tools such as virtual interactive whiteboards and screensharing. The pedagogical approach in these courses was to promote group work, collaboration, and problem-solving opportunities for students and interactive technologies were carefully integrated to foster active learning experiences. Ethics applications for the project were approved prior to data collection (Ethics approval numbers: H20REA133 and H20REA133v1).

Our studies were limited to exploring three interactive technologies, selected because they are free, easily accessible technologies that embed well across most learning management systems or videoconferencing software. *Padlet* (padlet.com) offers a virtual wall on which multimedia can be shared. Studies have shown that student experiences with Padlet were generally positive for student motivation, participation, cognitive engagement, and collaborative learning (Gill-Simmen, 2021; Mehta et al., 2021), although a limitation is that it can become unmanageable when overpopulated with content (Dianati et al., 2020). *Google Docs* (docs.google.com) is a suite of technological tools including a word processor, spreadsheet, presentation system, and forms. Google Docs can be accessed through a web browser, requires minimal training to use, and is useful for anonymous formative or summative assessments (Brigham, 2014; Serrano et al., 2019; Tran & Lamar, 2020) with identified challenges being students' lack of skill, formatting issues, and slow Internet connections. (Morrquin et al., 2019; Neumann & Kopcha, 2019; Suwantarathip & Wichadee, 2014). *Video-embedded quizzes* are quizzes that are embedded in pre-recorded videos using Panopto (panopto.com). Research shows that students tend not to skip over video-embedded quizzes (Kovacs, 2016), perhaps because they are interactive and give students purpose and motivation for paying more attention to videos (Cummins et al., 2016; Geri et al., 2017; Jones et al., 2021; Kenney & Fisher, 2017; Kimbrel & Gantner, 2021; Rice et al., 2019). However, it is not clear whether these quizzes help all students or just those with higher aptitudes (Lacher et al., 2018; MacKenzie & Ballard, 2015). All the practice examples shared in this Element draw from our work with these three technologies across the courses we have taught.

Each technology was either embedded in the learning management system or used in synchronous tutorials. When used in synchronous tutorials conducted via Zoom, Padlet, and Google Docs were shared for students to use as a class or in small groups in breakout rooms. Table 1 summarises how each technology was used across the mathematics and literacy courses.

As shown in Table 1, interactive technologies were used to enhance engagement and collaboration among pre-service teachers. Padlet facilitated anonymous sharing of feedback and reflections in mathematics tutorials, while in literacy courses, it was used to collect examples of children's language development and brainstorm tutorial activities. Google Docs supported group collaboration and problem-solving across both courses. Panopto video-embedded quizzes were integrated into short lecture videos to assess conceptual and theoretical understanding, with up to three quiz questions strategically placed within the recordings.

In summary, Padlet was used mainly for sharing ideas, resources, and anonymous feedback. It was employed live during Zoom sessions or within the learning management system for ongoing, asynchronous input. During the live Zoom sessions, Google Docs enabled real-time collaboration on problem-solving tasks and information compilation. These documents were also made accessible for students reviewing recorded tutorials later. In the lecture recordings, video-embedded quizzes were used to assess students' conceptual and theoretical knowledge, leveraging Panopto's capabilities to create interactive questions in various formats, including true/false, multiple-choice, multiple selections, and fill-in-the-blank, thereby enhancing learning engagement.

Data about interactive technologies and online student engagement were collected across our courses using pre- and post-surveys, learning analytics, and observations, as summarised in Table 2.

Table 1 How the interactive technologies were used in the courses

Technology	Mathematics courses	Literacy courses
Padlet	Gathering pre-service teachers' feedback and ideas anonymously about tutorial topics and reflections on lectures	Gathering pre-service teachers' examples of children's language and literacy learning and development and collating ideas for tutorial activities
Google Docs	Group collaboration and problem-solving activities	
Panopto video-embedded quizzes	Conceptual and theoretical knowledge checks. Brief (no more than 3) quiz questions embedded at the beginning, middle, or end of a 10- to 20-minute pre-recorded lecture video.	

Table 2 Summary of data collection

Method	Data	Details
Survey	The pre-service teachers' demographic information and experiences using Padlet, Google Docs, and video embedded quizzes (Likert scale) were collected.	Questions based on Redmond et al. (2018) Online Engagement Framework indicators.
Analytics	The numbers of pre-service teachers who participated in the embedded quizzes and Padlet activities were noted.	Learning management system reports and video-viewing analytics
Observation	The observation checklist rated pre-service teachers' engagement by watching video-recorded lessons.	Observation items based on Redmond et al. (2018) OEF indicators.

The use of three data sets ensured a holistic approach to engagement, not reliant on any one type of data. The particulars of the data collection tools can be found in our previous publications (Getenet & Tualaulelei, 2023; Getenet et al., 2022; Singh et al., 2023; Tualaulelei, 2020; Tualaulelei et al., 2021) but briefly:

- The pre- and post-surveys were administered online with the pre-survey conducted at the beginning of each course and the post-survey at the end.

The surveys gathered pre-service teachers' demographic data and their experiences and perspectives of using interactive technologies using a Likert scale ('Strongly disagree' to 'Strongly agree'). The survey questions were derived from the online engagement framework indicators (Redmond et al., 2018).

- Learning analytics were captured by the learning management system (LMS), Panopto video analytics, and Padlet usage statistics. The LMS reports quantified student participation, the number of times resources were accessed, for how long, and when. Panopto analytics captured the number of times lectures had been viewed, the number of pre-service teachers who participated in the embedded quizzes, their results, and overall quiz scores. Padlet statistics captured the number of posts, comments, reactions, and contributors for individual Padlets. Learning analytics data were used to supplement the data from the surveys and observations.
- Observations of video-recorded tutorials were conducted using a checklist based on the online engagement framework indicators (Redmond et al., 2018). The authors conducted observations for each course for a total of 483 minutes of tutorial activities using Padlet and Google Docs (Quiz use was not recorded because students completed these individually on their own time). The observations used the same online engagement indicators as those used in the survey from Redmond et al. (2018). Each indicator was checked with a yes or no response, and descriptions of examples were recorded when the indicators were present.
- Regarding data analysis, descriptive statistics were used to assess participants' agreement levels from the survey on engagement dimensions (social, cognitive, behavioural, and collaborative) in an online learning context. In addition, engagement was evaluated through an observation checklist by analysing video-recorded lessons to identify relevant aspects of engagement. A deductive quantitative count measured engagement levels by recording the frequency of occurrences for each dimension and explanations provided when applicable. The checklist also documented specific examples of engagement with descriptive details. Furthermore, participants in embedded quizzes and Padlet activities were identified using Panopto and Padlet web analytics, looking at counts and frequencies.

1.4 Outline of the Element

This section has defined student engagement in relation to online teacher education, delimited what we consider to be relevant interactive technologies, and described the research upon which this Element is based. The remaining sections present in-depth explorations of widely accepted dimensions of student engagement – cognitive, behavioural, affective, and other types of engagement. Each section begins with a concise summary of a dimension as it relates to online teacher education, followed by an explanation of how interactive technologies promote the dimension. These sections are followed by contextualised examples of practice from our previous studies described in Section 1.3 and a summary.

Section 2 focuses on *cognitive* engagement, where pre-service teachers demonstrate a deep understanding of the profession, justify their decision-making in relation to theories of teaching and learning, and think critically about all aspects of their professional role. While this dimension is necessarily prioritised in online education, it is not enough to develop the teacherly dispositions required by the teaching profession. Of course, we want teachers who are smart and intellectually engaged, but we also want teachers who are organised, who can communicate, and who are flexible and resourceful.

Section 3 discusses *behavioural* engagement, where pre-service teachers demonstrate the behaviours of engaged learners. This includes following conventions for academic writing and online learning, being agentic in their learning journey, and developing research, writing, and presentation skills. Behavioural engagement is often paired with cognitive engagement because each promotes the other. When students are behaviourally engaged, they are usually also cognitively engaged and vice versa. Like cognitive engagement, however, behavioural engagement alone is insufficient for teacher education because we do not want just teachers who are good at learning. Teaching is a relational and caring profession, so we also want teachers who understand the value of affective engagement.

Section 4 discuses *affective* engagement, which encompasses the emotional, motivational, and attitudinal aspects of engagement. This relates to a pre-service teacher's confidence in online learning and their identity as a teacher. It is concerned with their drive and commitment to learn and how much they enjoy learning about becoming a teacher. This section argues that affect can mediate behavioural and cognitive engagement, and we show how interactive technologies provide opportunities to promote these three types of engagement simultaneously.

Section 5 looks at other types of engagement beyond the three discussed, specifically exploring *social* and *collaborative* engagement. Social engagement is where pre-service teachers gain a sense of belonging and develop relationships with their online peers and faculty, whereas collaborative engagement is concerned with the relationships they nurture that will serve them beyond the university. These dimensions are, we argue, where interactive technologies become most effective. Cognitive, behavioural, and affective engagement can arise from non-interactive technologies if a pre-service teacher is sufficiently motivated; however, social and collaborative engagement is more likely to occur when using interactive technologies for communication with others.

Section 6 concludes this Element by asking where we go from here. We summarise what student engagement looked like for our pre-service teachers before discussing the challenges of using interactive technologies. The closing section explores the future possibilities of interactive technologies to 'grow' teachers online who can engage their own students.

2 Cognitive Engagement

In teacher education programmes the concept of 'cognitive engagement' has emerged as a critical component, especially in the context of the online learning environment. This section examines the importance of cognitive engagement in online teacher education, evaluating its significance and impact on engaging pre-service teachers in online learning. The discussion includes practical examples of how interactive technologies have been integrated in online teacher education programme settings to enhance cognitive engagement. In conclusion, key insights and takeaways are summarised to provide a comprehensive understanding of the strategies that promote cognitive engagement in online settings.

2.1 Cognitive Engagement in Online Teacher Education

Cognitive engagement refers to 'students' investment in learning key concepts and ideas and embracing of challenge in ways that go beyond minimum requirements' (Fletcher et al., 2018, p. 836). Cognitive engagement is core to most definitions of student engagement as it describes the effort that students are willing to put into their learning. Fredricks et al. (2004) described cognitive engagement in terms of 'thoughtfulness and willingness to exert the effort necessary to comprehend complex ideas and master difficult skills' (p. 60), suggesting that students play an agentic, rather than passive, role. It encompasses how students use their motivations and strategies during learning, integrating these elements into their educational journey (Richardson & Newby, 2018). It, therefore, involves learners participating in their learning process, showing an active interest that extends beyond the basic requirements of a class.

Cognitive engagement also happens at different levels, from surface through deep to metacognitive. Surface cognitive engagement is where learners engage at a minimal level. They might offer solutions, repeat ideas, or agree with others all without justification or clarification. As Redmond et al. (2018) wrote,

'Students who work at this level can easily be distracted, employ avoidance strategies, and focus on completing the task as a means to an end rather than learning from the task' (p. 192). In initial teacher education, this includes pre-service teachers who log into learning management systems minimally or put low effort into assessments. Learners can achieve more advanced intellectual development and expertise by focusing on skills like deep critical thinking and synthesising ideas beyond the surface level of cognition (Fredricks et al., 2004). This type of engagement may occur when learners construct and confirm meaning through sustained reflection and discourse in a learning community (Guo et al., 2014) and when learners integrate ideas from different sources or provide evidence to support their ideas. It can be observed when pre-service teachers discuss conceptual or theoretical ideas about teaching, and in case study group work, where individuals pool their ideas. Extending deep engagement, Richardson and Newby (2018) argued that the more cognitively engaged learners may even use 'metacognitive' skills to help them plan for learning and recognise how to better engage in learning. For example, learners may transpose lecture notes into formats that make more sense to them, or they may study at times when they can concentrate best. Self-regulation and self-efficacy are also considered metacognitive skills. Considering the definitions given earlier, deep and metacognitive engagements are clearly more desirable than surface engagement, so the use of interactive technologies and planned activities should aim to stimulate these levels of cognitive engagement.

The cognitive engagement of pre-service teachers matters in online teacher education for three reasons. First, pre-service teachers will encounter a wide range of educational theories, frameworks, pedagogies, approaches, ideas, and regularly updated policies and curricula throughout their degrees (Ravindran et al., 2005). Deep cognitive engagement will help them make connections across this information, even when it conflicts or changes, while metacognitive engagement will assist pre-service teachers to develop reflective capacities useful for studying and future teaching. Second, there is a public expectation that teachers are literate and numerate, and the profession is constantly under scrutiny due to school student performances in national and international tests (Goepel, 2012; Heffernan et al., 2019). In Australia, this scrutiny, in part, to the nationally mandated Literacy and Numeracy Test for Initial Teacher Education (LANTITE), ensuring that teachers were among the top 30 per cent of the population in terms of literacy and numeracy. Deep cognitive engagement means that during initial teacher education pre-service teachers continually develop their academic skills in ways that will support them later in-service professional development and uphold public trust in the teaching profession. Third, when pre-service teachers are cognitively engaged and experience academic success, they can better appreciate the efforts that their future students will make. Cognitive engagement adds a sense of meaningfulness to the efforts one puts into learning.

2.1.1 Indicators and Measures of Cognitive Engagement

A previous study by Zhu (2006) explored cognitive engagement in different online learning settings. With the notion that cognitive engagement is not observable in online learning, Zhu argued that cognitive engagement could be examined by analysing learners' behaviours of seeking, interpreting, analysing, and summarising information, critiquing and reasoning through various options and arguments, and making decisions in online discussions. Zhu (2006) further argued that high levels of cognitive engagement hold significant importance as they are closely linked to enhanced knowledge and skill development. This becomes especially crucial in an online learning environment, where synchronous dialogue opportunities between pre-service teachers, teachers, and peers are limited, and their cognitive engagement level is influenced by the amount and kind of effort the learners expend on classroom tasks (Richardson & Newby, 2018).

Similarly, Van der Meijden (2005) investigated cognitive engagement from the point of view of social knowledge construction, where learners' elaboration while constructing knowledge is evaluated in online discussions, and learners are categorised as cognitively engaged at either a low or high level. At the low level are those learners who primarily did not elaborate on their statements when constructing knowledge, while learners at the high level explained their facts and asked questions that triggered other questions. Hence, in online learning, understanding the role of cognitive presence in learning can help improve online teaching, and it is an essential indicator of positive learning outcomes for students (Wang & Stein, 2021).

Other researchers have proposed approaches to engagement theory for identifying and measuring cognitive engagement. For example, the theory proposed by Morris and Chi (2020) identified four levels of cognitive engagement: interactive, constructive, active, and passive. They argued that each engagement level results in more effective learning than the following one because it stimulates different, more generative, knowledge-change processes. In theory, learners' understanding is predicted to be better when the learner uses more effective processes such as selection, analysis, retrieval, elaboration, organisation, and integration of knowledge. For example, according to Chi (2021) and Morris and Chi (2020), *active* engagement is stimulated by tasks that require learners to focus on and manipulate lesson materials but not to generate anything beyond the provided materials. In *constructive* engagement tasks, students are stimulated to change the lesson materials to generate new knowledge, perhaps by making new connections, inferences, or predictions. The most cognitively engaging tasks require *interactive* engagement in which students work with others in constructive engagement mode, but in a manner that stimulates them to generate new connections beyond those generated by individual members of the group. Chi (2021) also refers to interactive engagement as involving co-constructive interaction (p. 455).

Specific to online teacher education, Redmond et al. (2018) suggested several key indicators of cognitive engagement gleaned from a survey of academic literature: thinking critically, activating metacognition, integrating ideas, justifying decisions, developing deep discipline understandings, and distributing expertise (p. 190). The authors highlighted that these indicators occur within disciplinary contexts, but they are transferable across disciplines. For preservice teachers especially, fostering cognitive engagement is essential as it enhances knowledge and skill development, particularly in online settings where direct interaction is limited. Effective engagement leads students to actively construct and synthesise knowledge, promoting deeper and more meaningful learning outcomes. Teachers play a key role in creating activities that encourage higher cognitive processes like analysis and problem-solving, which are vital for substantive learning experiences. Therefore, it is essential to develop professional knowledge in teacher education, requiring a level of cognitive engagement expected to be reflected in future teaching practices.

2.2 How Interactive Technologies Promote Cognitive Engagement

Interactive technologies play a central role in developing online learners' cognitive engagement (Attard & Holmes, 2020; Getenet & Tualaulelei, 2023; Getenet et al., 2022; Redmond et al., 2018). Previous studies (Attard & Holmes, 2020; Getenet & Tualaulelei, 2023; Redmond et al., 2018) and a systematic literature review (Schindler et al., 2017) have demonstrated that specific interactive technologies, such as social media networks and digital tools integrated into higher education learning systems, positively impact learner engagement, leading to more effective learning outcomes. These interactive technologies not only improve learners' digital skills but also provide flexible learning options tailored to learner preferences to keep them engaged in their learning (Lee & Martin, 2019). Despite these advantages, effectively utilising these technologies to promote learner engagement remains an ongoing challenge, given the continuous influx of new interactive technologies into the market (Schindler et al., 2017). Therefore, selectively implementing interactive technology is essential in online teaching to ensure improved engagement and learning experiences (Getenet & Tualaulelei, 2023; Getenet et al., 2022).

Specific interactive technologies, when used with care and planning, have shown promise for enhancing learners' engagement levels and motivation (Dianati et al., 2020; Getenet & Tualaulelei, 2023; Serrano et al., 2019). Blogs (Cakir, 2013; Özbek et al., 2023), synchronous tutorials through videoconferencing (Chigeza & Halbert, 2014), social media (Kabilan, 2016; Saini & Abraham, 2019), and ePortfolios (Chung & Jeong, 2024; Oakley et al., 2013) have been researched in the context of online teacher education. The technologies were beneficial for both independent and collaborative learning, and for enhancing learner motivation, effort, and participation. Most of these technologies have user-friendly interfaces and are cost-effective. Importantly, they promote deep cognitive engagement through, for example, peer-to-peer discussions and active knowledge construction. They also promote metacognitive engagement through individual and group reflections, goal setting, and documentation of learner progress. Lee et al. (2022) used flipped classrooms to enhance pre-service teachers' engagement in online learning by combining Zoom, recorded videos, and Google Classroom (classroom.google.com). In Lee and colleagues' (2022) study, before attending the Zoom synchronous class time, pre-service teachers were required to watch an educator's pre-recorded lectures and supplementary YouTube videos based on the course content. The pre-recorded videos were connected to a learning management system that allowed the educator to monitor and track each participant's completion of the materials. The synchronous Zoom also allowed the educator to incorporate various team-based collaborative activities, such as group discussion, lesson plans for technology integration, online micro-teaching, giving and receiving feedback sessions in Zoom breakout rooms, and crafting Google Classrooms. After a Zoom synchronous class, pre-service teachers were required to submit reflections based on the content covered each week. Using a combination of these technologies promoted active learning engagement through group discussions and collaborative team activities (Lee et al., 2022).

Across the literature, there is one factor that trumps any technology or teaching technique, and that is the online teacher educator and teaching mentors. The use of interactive technologies and the cognitive gains that learners derive from these are only as good as the intentions and planning of the teacher educator (Chan et al., 2021; Fletcher et al., 2018; Getenet & Tualaulelei, 2023). Research has also found that teaching mentors and in-service teachers can enhance pre-service teachers' cognitive engagement when studying online (Alwafi et al., 2020). For this reason, whichever technologies are selected, it is up to teacher educators to understand the benefits and drawbacks of using these and which types of cognitive engagement (surface, deep, or metacognitive) they seek to develop.

2.3 Practice Examples and Explanations of Impact

The examples that follow illustrate the principles discussed in previous sections, providing insights into how interactive technologies can enhance an online learner's cognitive engagement, utilising Redmond and colleagues' (2018) online engagement framework to assess their effectiveness. Pre-service teachers were engaged in various activities to enhance different indicators of cognitive engagement, such as activating their metacognition, integrating ideas, and justifying decisions.

Activating metacognition: Undergraduate pre-service teachers studying literacy were asked to collaboratively complete an anecdotal observation of a child's language and literacy development. A Padlet was set up with three columns – observations, interpretations, and implications – and together students viewed the video of a three-year-old child and entered information into each column. This was a practice activity for a planned assessment to be undertaken later. After the practice activity, the pre-service teachers reflected on what they learned from each other and how they could improve their ways of thinking (cognitive strategies) for the actual assessment.

Integrating ideas: To develop pre-service teachers' skills in integrating ideas, an activity was included in a mathematics education course. This activity invited students to activate their prior knowledge of teaching approaches for specific concepts. For example, one activity focused on the numeration system, which was the main topic of the tutorial. Pre-service teachers were also asked to reflect on how to teach this concept in a primary school context, as discussed in another course, and to share their reflections using Padlet. This activity encouraged them to combine their prior knowledge with newly acquired information and allowed them to learn from various teaching approaches used by their peers for teaching the numeration system in primary schools.

Justifying decisions: In a similar mathematics course, students were asked to make and justify a decision on competitive pricing, sharing their reasoning in a Google Document group. They were given two cases: Retailer A offered to beat the price of an identical item by 10 per cent, while Retailer B offered to refund 110 per cent of the difference. Based on these scenarios, students were asked to reflect on the question, 'What is the power in the number being quoted by Retailer A and Retailer B in attracting customers?' and provide specific examples. This type of activity helped pre-service teachers to engage cognitively, particularly in developing their skills in justifying decisions.

Table 3 Interactive technologies, number of pre-service teachers involved (N), topics taught, and activity description

No	Technology	N	Topic	Activity description
1	Padlet	20	Numeration system	Reflect on various numeration systems and their experiences at schools
2	Padlet	12	Teachers' knowledge of teaching mathematics with technology	Reflect and comment on various forms of teachers' knowledge for teaching mathematics
3	Google Docs	15	Learning mathematics with technology	Identify sum, mean, and generate graphs to identify the best technology for teaching a specific mathematics concept
4	Google Docs	8	Problem based learning for effective mathematics teaching	Solve problems by posting pictures, generating graphs and calculations from the provided data

To demonstrate the impact of interactive technologies on pre-service teachers' cognitive engagement, Table 3 presents an overview of their use in a mathematics course, detailing the number of pre-service teachers involved, topics covered, and activities conducted. It lists four entries: two using Padlet with 20 and 12 pre-service teachers, focusing on numeration systems and teachers' knowledge in math technology, involving reflective activities. The other two activities used Google Docs with 15 and 8 pre-service teachers, exploring mathematical concepts through practical tasks like graph generation and problem-solving activities.

In a post-course survey, twelve pre-service teachers out of ninety participants responded, and Table 4 summarises the cognitive engagement levels of participants measured across three digital tools – Google Docs, Padlet, and Panopto – for three indicators: thinking critically, developing a deep understanding of the discipline, and using expertise gained from other courses.

As shown in Table 4 and examining specific indicators, the technologies received similar mean scores. Table 5 compares learners' cognitive engagement in Google Docs and Padlet focusing on these same indicators.

Table 4 Participants' cognitive engagement scores: means and standard deviations

Indicator	Google Doc	Padlet	Panopto
Thinking critically	3.19 (0.97)	3.28 (1.14)	3.44 (0.11)
Developing a deep discipline understanding	3.13 (0.87)	3.19 (1.15)	3.47 (1.14)
Using expertise gained from other courses	3.22 (1.00)	3.25 (1.11)	3.28 (0.99)

Table 5 Pre-service teachers' cognitive engagement in Padlet and Google Docs and the observed frequencies

Indicators	Google Docs (N)	Padlet (N)	Descriptive example
Think critically	11	5	*Google Docs:* Pre-service teachers discussed critical ideas while interpreting the data provided. *Padlet:* To craft responses to questions
Develop a deep, discipline understanding	13	6	*Google Docs*: Raised and answered questions about data *Padlet*: Represent a number using a different number system
Use expertise gained from other courses	7	3	*Google Docs and Padlet*: Drew upon previous mathematics courses to answer questions.

The findings shown in Table 5 underscore the multifaceted contributions of both Padlet and Google Docs to diverse aspects of pre-service teachers' cognitive engagement, signifying the nuanced ways these tools interact with student participation and motivation within the learning process. For example, for critical thinking, Google Docs with 11 occurrences shows a higher frequency than Padlet with a frequency of 5. This is exemplified by pre-service teachers discussing critical ideas and interpreting data, representing numbers using different number systems, and exploring how these concepts might be taught effectively in primary schools. Meanwhile, Padlet users crafted responses to questions, and other findings highlighted the varying levels of pre-service teachers' cognitive engagement, with Padlet fostering active and participatory learning environments. For example, in one course Padlet, there were 123 posts,

20 comments, 45 reactions, and 50 contributors, indicating moderate engagement. Through this platform, pre-service teachers used technology to support reflecting on the necessary knowledge for teaching mathematics and how these requirements manifest in classroom settings. Both technologies supported pre-service teachers in developing disciplinary knowledge such as mathematical concepts and understanding effective teaching methods for these concepts.

2.4 Summary

This section has explored the role of interactive technology in enhancing cognitive engagement within online teacher education. We began by defining 'cognitive engagement' in the context of online learning, emphasising its importance as a construct that encompasses student motivation, depth of processing, and active involvement in learning activities. Moving forward, we explored how interactive technologies can be useful in promoting cognitive engagement. These technologies, ranging from collaborative tools to virtual classrooms, facilitate dynamic interaction, deeper understanding, and active participation, enhancing learners' learning experience. Practical examples were provided to illustrate the effective integration of these technologies in educational settings. By effectively understanding and implementing these technologies, educators can create more engaging, interactive, and effective learning experiences for pre-service teachers, ultimately contributing to their professional growth and readiness for the dynamic demands of modern classrooms. These examples demonstrated how interactive tools engage pre-service teachers cognitively and foster an environment conducive to higher-order thinking, problem-solving, and meaningful learning. By leveraging the potential of interactive technologies to enhance cognitive engagement, we can better prepare pre-service teachers for the complexities of contemporary online education. This approach enriches their learning experience and equips them with the skills and knowledge necessary for teaching.

3 Behavioural Engagement

Pre-service teachers join online teacher education programmes with different knowledge, experiences, and skills that need to be further developed for contemporary learning. This section describes the concept of 'behavioural engagement', its role, and its effects on engaging learners in the context of online teacher education. It showcases how interactive technology-enhanced learning environments can foster this type of engagement. The section showcases practical examples where interactive technologies have been successfully integrated to enhance behavioural engagement and ends with a summary of key insights.

3.1 Behavioural Engagement in Online Teacher Education

Different authors have variously defined behavioural engagement but is broadly characterised by positive conduct, involvement in academic tasks, and participation in school activities (Fredricks et al., 2004). The conceptual structure and theory of student behavioural engagement are largely derived from studies of traditional classroom teaching, though they present differently and might not be as explicit and observable in online learning contexts. Supporting this, Hu and Li (2017) argued that in online learning, learners' behavioural engagement is important, but it is difficult to define clearly and cannot fully reflect the learners' efforts. Recently, researchers have categorised student behavioural engagement into two types: activities conducted inside the classroom and those performed outside of it (Ranellucci et al., 2021; Wang, 2019). This categorisation includes online activities as a part of out-of-class engagement. Furthermore, when students actively participate in online platforms for their learning, this specific interaction is identified as their engagement in online learning (Ranellucci et al., 2021; Wang, 2019). In a traditional environment, the study of behavioural engagement relies on observation of student responses to physical and verbal cues provided by the teacher; however, these responses become less observable in the online environment, where students do not necessarily engage directly with their teachers and peers as part of the learning process (Lei et al., 2019). Visual indicators of physical engagement in online learning are not as evident as in face-to-face learning (Lei et al., 2019). Rather, in an online context, student–content interactions become the key indicators of student behavioural engagement but seldom provide sufficient information for understanding how students regulate their behaviour or why they behave as they do (Al Mamun & Lawrie, 2023). This makes defining and measuring behavioural engagement in online learning more challenging.

3.1.1 Indicators and Measures of Behavioural Engagement

Defining and measuring students' behavioural engagement in an online learning environment requires a different lens from the one used in a traditional classroom where a teacher can directly observe student behaviour. Vytasek et al. (2020) suggested that students' digital artefacts can be used to infer their behavioural engagement. Existing studies have applied behavioural sequence analysis to investigate users' behavioural engagement during social interactions in an online learning context (Sun et al., 2017). Sung et al. (2018) also found, through analysing behavioural patterns, that higher achieving learners performed more deep-strategy behaviours during the learning process. One example of such methodology is the use of computer-sourced data about learner activity, including time spent in the learning management system, number of logins, number of transactions, content completion rate, completed test rate, number of questions answered correctly, and numbers of forum posts and comments as indicators of engagement in the online learning environment (Antonaci et al., 2019; Hew et al., 2016). Similarly, through correlation and regression analysis, Li et al. (2016) explored the relationships of thirteen indicators of behavioural engagement with online learning performance. Their results showed that online learning behavioural engagement significantly correlates with learning performance and indicators of learning performance. These thirteen indicators were:

> logon numbers, time spent on the platform, average time spent on the platform of each logon, rate of announcements read, number of completed topics, number of videos watched incompletely, number of videos watched completely, number of videos without being watched, number of lesson quizzes taken, time of taking lesson quizzes, average times of attempting to do lesson quizzes, number of completed units and number of completed lessons. (Li et al., 2016, p. 248)

Highlighting various studies, Pan (2023) supplemented the concept of learning behavioural engagement by putting forward categories and measuring indexes, namely, participation, interaction, persistence, concentration, academic challenge, and self-directed learning.

Other studies have adopted multiple frameworks and suggested strategies for measuring learner behavioural engagement in videos. For example, Bote-Lorenzo and Gómez-Sánchez (2017) pointed out sixteen indicators specifically for gauging behavioural engagement in online courses. Similarly, Li and Tsai (2017) focused on fourteen indicators tied to the time students dedicate to educational materials, including videos. Moreover, metrics like the number of views or clicks, viewing time length/duration, and viewing completion rate and frequency have been used to assess students' behavioural engagement, as noted by researchers such as Breslow et al. (2013), Guo et al. (2014), and Jordan (2014). In the context of online learning in higher education, and from a survey of academic literature, Redmond et al. (2018) suggested developing academic skills, identifying opportunities and challenges, developing multidisciplinary skills, developing agency, upholding online learning norms, and supporting and encouraging peers as indicators and measures of behavioural engagement.

Understanding the concept and indicators of learning behavioural engagement and experience in teacher education programmes is essential for pre-service teachers, as it enables them to identify engaged learners, intervene early with disengaged students, and personalise learning experiences (Darling-Aduana, 2019). This awareness helps motivate pre-service teachers, helps them make informed technological choices, and informs their lesson design for improved learning outcomes. Developing skills in recognising behavioural engagement patterns supports pre-service teachers' and educators' professional development, ensuring they are equipped to foster dynamic and inclusive learning environments. As a result, within the context of teacher education, pre-service teachers' behavioural engagement is not only important for their own learning but also might affect their future teaching practices. As suggested by Saini and Abraham (2019), pre-service teachers who are provided with experiences in behaviourally engaged learning environments are more likely to use similar approaches in their teaching practices in schools.

3.2 How Interactive Technologies Promote Behavioural Engagement

Research shows clear correlations between technology-enhanced learning and behavioural engagement (Li et al., 2016; Sung et al., 2018), although it also indicates that not all technologies are effective in fostering the engagement of online learners (Getenet & Tualaulelei, 2023).

Taşkın and Kılıç Çakmak (2022) created a learning environment supported by gamification to enhance learners' behavioural engagement by attracting their attention to the content presented for learning. In this game-based learning environment, to complete the course, learners were required to perform several interrelated tasks for which they were awarded, such as logging in watching a video, solving an assessment task, or examining a presentation. By rewarding students with points for activities like logging in, completing courses, or passing tests, and requiring a mix of tasks (videos, infographics, tests, presentations) for course completion, this method effectively draws attention to the learning material and encourages learners' behavioural engagement. It demonstrated how gamified elements can make online learning more interactive and engaging, suggesting a practical model for educators to improve behavioural engagement and learning outcomes.

In English teaching, Hafour and Alwaleedi (2022) explored the impact of cloud-based collaborative writing on pre-service teachers' behavioural engagement by utilising cloud learning analytics tools. Google Docs was used as a tool for collaborative writing, allowing pre-service teachers to work together on texts by adding, substituting, deleting, or rearranging text elements, as well as engaging in collaboration around texts using commenting features and chat rooms. Furthermore, the research highlighted collaboration through text, where pre-service teachers used written language to communicate. According to Hafour and Alwaleedi (2022), the learning analytics system measured pre-service teachers' behavioural engagement and showed their improved engagement when using Google Docs. The use of these cloud-based collaborative tools highlighted a key takeaway for teachers and pre-service teachers, that student behavioural engagement can be improved through features that enable collaboration and interaction. This research also showcases the importance of learning analytics in understanding behavioural engagement patterns. Educators are encouraged to adopt technologies that promote active learning and use analytics to effectively tailor their teaching strategies, preparing for more interactive and engaging learning environments.

Social media has also been used to improve pre-service teachers' behavioural engagement. Saini and Abraham (2019) used Facebook to enhance pre-service teachers' behavioural engagement in a teacher education programme. Initially, an open group was formed on Facebook, and kept open for a short period so that the pre-service teachers could easily locate and join it. The privacy setting was then changed to 'closed' group so that only the intended pre-service teachers could participate in group activities. Despite the familiarity of pre-service teachers with Facebook, they were provided with orientation about acceptable practices on Facebook and how to use Facebook features in academic contexts. The activities began with a brief face-to-face introduction by the researcher, followed by set tasks (individual/group) that ranged from locating and sharing relevant content to comprehending the content and taking part in online discussions and quizzes, through problem-solving to the analysis of case studies, watching online videos, and participating in online polls. These activities provided opportunities for pre-service teachers to learn how to construct knowledge in a shared environment and enhance their engagement. The findings indicated that integrating social media such as Facebook into teacher education courses can enhance pre-service teachers' behavioural engagement and achievement. This suggests that teachers can effectively use social media, with appropriate orientation and structured activities, to foster a productive learning environment and learning behavioural engagement in their future teaching.

Recently, Gameil and Al-Abdullatif (2023) conducted a comprehensive review of studies on the Google Classroom platform, focusing on its impact on teaching efficiency, academic achievement, and the engagement of pre-service teachers. Google Classroom is a digital learning platform designed to assist teachers in creating engaging educational experiences, enabling learners to conveniently access materials, interact with peers, frequently utilise learning resources, and enjoy the flexibility to study from any location at any time. Their findings indicate that Google Classroom has a positive effect on improving learners' behavioural engagement and performance. For teachers, this underscores the value of integrating Google Classroom or similar platforms into their educational practices. By doing so, they can enhance learning experiences, facilitate access to materials, and support interaction, contributing to better student outcomes.

Lecture videos have become increasingly popular in higher education to supplement or replace traditional in-person lectures in online learning. However, ensuring that students remain engaged while watching them is challenging. To address this issue, some educators have begun incorporating interactive elements, such as quizzes, into their lecture videos to improve students' behavioural engagement and learning outcomes. In our recent studies (Getenet & Tualaulelei, 2023; Getenet et al., 2022), we explored the use of video-embedded quizzes to enhance pre-service teachers' engagement, including behavioural engagement. These quizzes prompted pre-service teachers to pause and answer questions on the covered material, thereby encouraging active engagement with the content. Our findings revealed that integrating interactive quizzes in lecture videos not only increased pre-service teachers' motivation to complete viewing these videos but also led to better behavioural engagement and performance. This method offers a valuable strategy for educators to enhance online learning by making it more interactive and effective, emphasising the importance of incorporating engaging elements into digital teaching materials.

3.3 Practice Examples and Explanations of Impact

Exploring various indicators of behavioural engagement and the activities that facilitate flourishing in the classroom is important for supporting learning engagement. The following cases are examples of activities designed to support pre-service teachers' behavioural engagement across various indicators from Redmond et al. (2018).

Identifying opportunities and challenges: A valued skill in teaching is the ability to identify one's own professional learning needs. In a post-graduate literacy course, teachers completed quiz questions during videos that tested their knowledge of five systems of language – phonology, morphology, syntax, semantics, and pragmatics. The quiz results helped pre-service teachers identify weaknesses in their content knowledge and seek suitable sources for professional development of these areas for an assessment task.

Developing multidisciplinary skills: In a mathematics education course, small groups of pre-service teachers were assigned separate tabs on Google Sheets for an activity where each group was asked to design paper planes with different sizes. After flying each plane five times, the groups recorded the distances travelled, calculated the mean for the distances, and summarised their investigation by identifying which size plane travelled the longest distance and explaining why. Each group was able to access the other groups' calculations online for comparison. These activities helped pre-service teachers to develop their skills in using technology, sharing ideas, and learning mathematical concepts online through interactive technologies like Google Sheets.

Supporting and encouraging peers: In small group work centred around Google Sheets, pre-service teachers were commonly observed assisting and supporting others with technology and online resources, especially when a more knowledgeable peer would support a less knowledgeable one. At times, particularly around assignment periods, students would begin to feel anxious or stressed and peers would help by offering advice with study tips, support services they had used at the university or advice with 'what not to do' from their own experiences. When arranging break-out rooms for small group activities, teacher educators can purposefully arrange groups including learners with various levels of technological knowledge or university experience to promote a supportive and encouraging group dynamic online.

In a survey we conducted measuring aspects of behavioural engagement, responses identified video quizzes as strongly enhancing behavioural engagement compared with Google Docs and Padlet (see Table 6), particularly in terms of developing academic skills, developing learner agency, and helping learners understand online norms.

In addition, observational data presented further insights. Examples of behavioural engagement promoted by Google Docs included the development of academic skills such as finding resources, conducting focused discussions, developing presentation and technology skills, and managing time. In one tutorial, the educator helped resolve pre-service teachers' problems with formatting, providing pre-service teachers with transferable skills they can use

Table 6 How the technologies facilitated behavioural engagement[a]

Indicators[b]	Google Docs		Padlet		Panopto quizzes	
	Pre[c]	Post	Pre	Post	Pre	Post
Develop academic skills	3.38	3.50	3.00	2.87	3.24	4.00
Develop agency	3.24	3.50	3.00	3.13	3.24	4.00
Understand online learning norms	3.38	3.50	2.94	3.00	3.24	4.13

[a] Getenet and Tualaulelei, 2023, p. 227
[b] Mean scores on Likert scale: Strongly agree = 5, Agree = 4, Neutral = 3, Disagree = 2, Strongly disagree = 1
[c] Pre-test $N = 28$, Post-test $N = 8$

with other word processing applications. Pre-service teachers were also observed supporting and encouraging their peers. Student agency, one of the indicators of behavioural engagement, was also observed, particularly after pre-service teachers had become accustomed to using the Google Docs technology; pre-service teachers were seen selecting or self-nominating leaders of the activity, and when the time was about to run out, pre-service teachers took the initiative to progress the activity.

Our findings underscore the necessity of understanding and integrating effective interactive technologies into pre-service teachers' learning experiences, focusing on those that foster academic skills, agency, and familiarity with online learning norms. Teacher educators, on the other hand, should consider the findings as a prompt to adapt and refine their teaching practices, leveraging tools like interactive quizzes to enhance learners' behavioural engagement. A practical approach enhances pre-service teachers' behavioural engagement and helps prepare them with the skills needed for the digital age.

3.4 Summary

Behavioural engagement in online teacher education is a vital component of the learning process, encompassing participation, effort, and involvement in academic tasks and learning activities. The shift to online learning environments has challenged traditional notions of behavioural engagement, requiring adaptations to measure student engagement through interactions with online learning platforms. Interactive technologies can support group work, collaboration, and active learning, demonstrating their effectiveness in promoting behavioural engagement among learners. However, educators must be aware of the various technologies available and be selective with the technologies they use, choosing those most responsive to their learners' specific needs and contexts. This awareness also supports professional development, equipping educators with the skills to foster dynamic and inclusive learning spaces that motivate students and improve academic outcomes.

4 Affective Engagement

One of the challenges for pre-service teachers studying online is to stay motivated, find joy in their learning, and feel an emotional connection to what they are learning, ideas that are collectively known as 'affective engagement'. This section explores and explains affective engagement as essential to successful teaching and learning because it humanises a process that is more than just cognitive and behavioural. The section then explores how interactive technologies promote pre-service teachers' affect in areas including motivation and commitment, enjoyment, and interest. Through personally experiencing the joy of learning, pre-service teachers are better equipped to promote this amongst their own students. The section then offers examples of how interactive technologies can be used to positively influence affective engagement. We will argue throughout that affective engagement complements, and to some extent, mediates the cognitive and behavioural dimensions discussed in the previous sections. The section concludes with a summary of key insights and takeaways.

4.1 Affective Engagement in Online Teacher Education

In education, affective engagement refers to the range of feelings and attitudes that learners have towards their studies. This differs from psychological research where 'affect' refers specifically to emotions and moods. Encompassing a range of attitudinal, emotional, and relational skills and dispositions, affective engagement is important for the teaching profession because there is evidence that it is connected to student achievement (Keller et al., 2016; Zee & Koomen, 2016). Just as importantly, affective engagement has been linked to teachers' enjoyment of the profession. Delamarter and Wiederholt (2019) surveyed 112 pre-service teachers in the United States of America, and found that 'affective/relational' outcomes from teacher education programmes were considered more important to the pre-service teachers than academic/intellectual outcomes. They wrote that 'this skew towards the affective lies in contrast with the formal evaluation measures used by many [initial teacher] programs today' (p. 143). Similarly, Holzberger et al. (2021) explored the characteristics of 649 German teacher candidates at the end of their initial teacher education and again 2 years into their teaching careers. They found that teacher mindset, which included motivation, self-efficacy, and enthusiasm, amongst other constructs, was positively linked to occupational well-being and teacher retention. In other words, teachers who are affectively engaged with initial teacher education are more likely to be affectively engaged *and engaging* as teachers. What has become increasingly clear is that initial teacher education must have a balance in emphasis towards, on one hand, academic or intellectual outcomes, and on the other, affective and relational outcomes.

Affect can influence pre-service teachers in different ways while they are studying online. Those with positive affect towards their educational experiences are more likely to succeed than those who experience negative affect (Fredricks et al., 2004). Some examples of positive constructs are enjoyment, motivation, pride, enthusiasm, interest, satisfaction, and a sense of well-being or positivity towards learning. Affect generally includes non-cognitive constructs. It is thought to be underpinned by the values and beliefs that pre-service teachers hold about their education – if they feel that what they are learning is important or necessary for their future goals and job security, they may persist in their studies during times when they experience negative affect (Audrin & Hascoët, 2024; Murdoch & Lim, 2022). Affect, however, also includes negative constructs such as disinterest, boredom, frustration, anxiety, or feeling excluded. When pre-service teachers experience negative affect, this can lead to disengagement and withdrawal from studying. Both positive and negative affect may be experienced in response to the course, its facilitators, and/or other participants. It may also be in response to a specific subject matter, the discipline or profession itself, or the institution delivering the course (Redmond et al., 2018). Affect clearly plays a role in whether pre-service teachers invest effort towards cognitive and behavioural engagement in their learning.

Some affective factors are more prominent than others in the research literature. Motivation is a key affective factor because it is thought to lead to active and sustained efforts at learning (Cho et al., 2021; Ferrer et al., 2022; Keller et al., 2016). When students are motivated, this may also shape their cognitive engagement (that is, deepen their learning) and behavioural engagement (that is, they take steps to learn how to get better at learning, which flows back into increasing their affective engagement). In short, the better pre-service teachers get at studying education, the more they enjoy it. This is important for teachers across their career-span because a great part of teaching is to engage with continued professional learning and development.

Emotional intelligence has also been posited as a key affective factor, as much of teaching is social, where emotions play a role in relating with others (Corcoran & Tormey, 2012; Hawkey, 2006). This is why an instructor's presence is valued in online learning environments. They can model emotional intelligence, create opportunities to develop it, and help moderate pre-service teachers' emotions when conflicts or disagreements arise online. Another oft-mentioned idea in the affective engagement literature is enjoyment or well-being within a course. This is captured in student satisfaction surveys about courses. Studies have shown that enjoyment is related to how the instructor communicates, how the course is laid out, and the types of activities they are asked to engage with (Hamsher & Dieterich, 2017). Motivation, emotional intelligence, and enjoyment are the most researched aspects of affect, but many other ideas may be categorised as 'affective engagement', depending on the teaching and cultural contexts.

Like cognitive and behavioural engagement, affective engagement is not a clearly delineated category in the academic literature about student engagement. It is known by various names depending on what researchers have focused upon, for example, emotional engagement (Redmond et al., 2018), personal engagement (Moss & Pittaway, 2018), the affective/relational domain (Delamarter & Wiederholt, 2019), to name a few. It has been suggested that when learners feel that learning activities afford them agency and match with their sense of self-efficacy, they are more likely to be interested in and enjoy learning (Reeve & Tseng, 2011). However, the precise roles of agency and self-efficacy and their relationship to affective engagement are unclear in the literature (Bond et al., 2020). The role of belonging is also unclear; if pre-service teachers feel that they belong in the teaching profession and in the institutes that educate teachers, is there a higher likelihood that they will enjoy their studies? And how about factors that co-relate, for example, hope and hopelessness, pride and shame, and so on? Interconnections between the different constructs that are categorised as 'affective' have not yet been fully explored.

We do know that for pre-service teachers, particularly those from diverse backgrounds or with diverse learning needs, affective engagement can mean the difference between success and failure with online education. In Australia, those studying initial teacher education online are typically female, mature-aged, from lower socio-economic backgrounds, and geographically located in regional, rural, or remote areas (Australian Institute for Teaching and School Leadership, 2018). Teaching is a highly feminised profession – in Australia, around 70 per cent of primary and secondary teachers and around 90 per cent of early years educators are female (Australian Institute for Teaching and School Leadership, 2023a; Education Services Australia, 2021). Stone and O'Shea (2019) have noted how mature-aged women who often carry an additional burden of care for their families, value an online culture of encouragement and support, making affective engagement particularly important. In an earlier study, the same authors found that students who were the first in their family to attend university were often highly motivated, but needed 'support to build their confidence and to gain experience of the demands and requirements of university' (Stone et al., 2016, p. 164). The participants in their study talked about the value of overcoming self-doubt, being grateful for the opportunity to study, and their hopes and educational aspirations; all these ideas highlight the importance of affective engagement. The challenge for online teacher educators is to identify the various aspects of affective engagement they wish to promote and to respond with suitable online teaching and learning activities.

4.1.1 Indicators and Measures of Affective Engagement

The indicators and measures of affective engagement vary across studies. In some studies, affect is tied in with other constructs such as motivation, for example, 'motivational-affective' (Holzberger et al., 2021), while other studies include aspects of self-efficacy, self-regulation, or persistence (Cho et al., 2021; Murdoch & Lim, 2022; Zee & Koomen, 2016). In a meta-analysis of synchronous online learning and affective educational outcomes, Martin et al. (2021) included in 'affective outcomes': 'learner satisfaction, emotions, attitudes, motivation and other measures' (p. 214). Affect is, therefore, an umbrella term that includes a variable set of indicators depending on the field and focus of the study. No matter what approach is taken to affect, it is generally accepted that 'the affective enables the academic', so it should not be emphasised over the academic (Delamarter & Wiederholt, 2019). In other words, enjoyment of a class should occur in parallel with academic learning.

Scholarship from the last decade has used quite broad descriptors for the indicators of affect. In a systematic review of 243 studies, among which 163 reported on affective engagement, Bond et al. (2020) noted five most often identified indicators for affective engagement: positive interaction with teachers and peers, enjoyment, positive attitude about learning interest, motivation, and enthusiasm. They also noted disengagement indicators, with the top five being: frustration, disappointment, worry/anxiety, boredom, and disinterest. Similarly, Daher et al. (2021) linked positive and negative affect to a framework from Bolliger and Martin (2018) as summarised in Table 7.

Other studies take a less dichotomised view of affect. Ferrer et al. (2022), for example, characterised affect in terms of attitude, specifically 'students' feelings towards their ability to use online technology to enhance learning' (p. 322), while Audrin and Hascoët (2024) found that joy was positively related to pre-service teachers' propensity to persist with teaching, but anger and anxiety were not significant influences. Data for these indicators are commonly captured through surveys and questionnaires (e.g., Anderson & Simpson, 2004; Audrin & Hascoët,

Table 7 Summary of affective indicators

	Interaction between the learner and other learners	Interaction between the learner and the teacher	Interaction between the learner and content
Positive affect	Comfort	Being interested	Not feeling the passing of time
Negative affect	Anxiety	Being uncomfortable	Feeling that time is not passing

2024; Schindler et al., 2017). Given these wide variations in how studies characterise affect, caution should be applied when comparing studies and interpreting findings without unpacking the construct of affect into its parts.

4.2 How Interactive Technologies Promote Affective Engagement

There is a wide variety of interactive technologies that online teacher educators can employ to promote positive affective engagement. In a systematic review of academic literature about online initial teacher education, Dyment and Downing (2019) found a 'wide diversity of synchronous and asynchronous innovations researched including, but not limited to, web conferences, discussion boards, chat rooms, instant messaging, digital games, social media, virtual laboratories, virtual simulators ... portfolios, and Facebook' (p. 326). In a critical review of the literature about technologies and general student engagement, Schindler et al. (2017) identified that the five most common technologies for supporting constructivist, interactive learning were web-conferencing, blogs, wikis, social networking sites (Facebook, Twitter), and digital games. With new technologies emerging frequently, teacher educators are spoilt for choice. However, the selection of tools for use by online educators is mediated by both their own technological skills and those of their students (Kordrostami & Seitz, 2021). For this reason, teacher educators should use technologies that provide a suitable amount of challenge but are not so complicated that they overwhelm learners and distract from teaching and learning goals.

The academic literature is inconclusive about the role of instructor interactions in promoting affective engagement. Hamsher and Dieterich (2017) surveyed 59 undergraduate and postgraduate students in initial teacher education and asked how instructors created a positive online learning atmosphere. They found that students valued instructors' 'logistical behaviours' over 'emotional-relational behaviours'. For example, the pre-service teachers valued clear directions and constructive feedback over interpersonal relationships with the instructor and humour in teaching. The implication is that instructors' dispositions, while important, are less valued than organisational and communicative skills. This contrasts with studies which point to the value of peer and teacher interactions for enhancing affect (Bedenlier et al., 2020; Burke et al., 2022; Cho et al., 2021). We have found that a combination of clear communication about the purpose and process of any activity using interactive technology, as well as a positive teaching disposition works well for promoting positive affect.

Evidence has also been found for a slight difference in educational outcomes for synchronous and asynchronous online activities (Martin et al., 2021), and students are typically drawn to the activities that suit their own purposes and needs (Tualaulelei et al., 2021). Given the subjectivity of many of the components included in 'affect', online teacher educators are best advised to combine synchronous and asynchronous activities and to vary learning activities to cater for different affective needs.

Technologies such as Padlet increase learners' motivation and effort because they are intuitive to use, visually appealing, and collaborative (Dianati et al., 2020). When configured appropriately, Padlet offers anonymity for users which is appealing for some learners (Deni & Zainal, 2018; Mehta et al., 2021). It can help pre-service teachers to build up their confidence in the online learning environment. Padlet can also be used as an inclusive teaching tool, with benefits reported for those with hearing impairments (DeWitt et al., 2015) and non-native English speakers (Arif et al., 2020; Ellis, 2015). Padlet is also useful as a tool for reflection (Shaw, 2023) because much of what pre-service teachers experience as affective engagement is based upon their beliefs and values. Reflection through Padlet can help pre-service teachers express these and gain a fuller understanding of their own teaching philosophies and approaches (Shaw, 2023). This can increase their confidence as pre-service teachers and motivate them to study.

The collaborative nature of the teaching profession means that applications like Google Docs can aid in the promotion of positive affect. Most learners are familiar with Google Docs due to its similarity to suites of office apps (e.g., Microsoft Office, Apple's iWork), so there is little to no training needed to use it. Google Docs' ease of use and accessibility make it suitable for time-poor online pre-service teachers, particularly those still familiarising themselves with using technology for learning. Real-time collaboration and problem-solving using Google's Education online apps gives learners a sense of community and ownership of the work they create in class (Heggart & Yoo, 2018; Morrquin et al., 2019). These features offer pre-service teachers a feeling of achievement and agency, as well as help them develop a sense of responsibility and commitment to their learning. Furthermore, Google Docs activities can promote group discussion (Tran & Lamar, 2020) and help strengthen peer-to-peer and peer-to-instructor relationships (McKnight et al., 2016). These social connections can help pre-service teachers develop a sense of professional identity as they get to know their online peers who may be potential future colleagues. Further, the social aspect of learning can contribute to feelings of well-being, inclusion, and overall satisfaction in a course. When learners experience these positive emotions, they can better direct their energies towards cognitive, behavioural, and other dimensions of engagement.

As outlined in Sections 2 and 3, video-embedded quizzes contribute strongly to pre-service teachers' cognitive and behavioural engagement and they can also support affective engagement. Receiving immediate feedback from video-embedded quizzes can enhance learners' satisfaction because pre-service teachers value timely and constructive feedback (Hamsher & Dieterich, 2017; Rice et al., 2019). The interactivity learners experience is quite different from what they experience with Padlet and Google Docs; with video-embedded quizzes, learners interact with pre-set questions, answers, and feedback, with possibilities to move forward or backward to a point in the video depending on the quiz result. Quizzes are, therefore, useful for maintaining pre-service teachers' interest in recorded lectures and motivating them to view video resources actively instead of passively.

Although this section has so far outlined ways to use interactive technologies to promote positive affect, it is also worth considering the use of these technologies to actively counter dimensions of negative affect (disinterest, boredom, frustration, anxiety, feeling excluded, etc.). In a study meant to identify helpful or practical uses of digital technology in online learning, Henderson et al. (2015) discovered that a relatively limited set of digital tools and practices was being used by instructors in online courses. While this can be partly attributed to institutions and the digital infrastructure made available for instructors and students, it can also be attributed to instructor practices and willingness to try new technologies. The remainder of the section details how we successfully implemented interactive technologies to promote affective engagement in our teacher education courses.

4.3 Practice Examples and Explanations of Impact

In this section, we explain how affective engagement was measured and the impacts of the interactive technologies on various aspects of pre-service teachers' affective engagement, specifically fostering belonging, trust, well-being, and enjoyment, commitment to learning, reflective dispositions, and countering negative affect.

Fostering Belonging

In a first-year literacy teaching course for early years education (birth to eight years), pre-service teachers explored how children learn language and literacy in the earliest years of life. The teachers were encouraged to collect samples of children's early language and literacy onto a Padlet that was embedded in the learning management system on the main page of the course. The samples were later analysed in online tutorials to demonstrate key literacy concepts and ideas, for example, the development of babies' communicative skills, the role of parents and caregivers in language and literacy learning, and the connections between children's early mark-making and later writing skills. Throughout the 15-week course, this Padlet was the most-viewed course resource and students continued to submit samples to the Padlet and comment after tutorial activities had ended. The high number of Padlet views showed that students were engaged with their online learning community and that the Padlet served as a valuable resource, fostering active participation and promoting interaction among students.

In terms of affective engagement, this Padlet activity helped students feel a sense of belonging to the course. Some pre-service teachers contributed samples from their children or the children they worked with. This added a personal dimension to the activity, which aroused interest and offered a sense of ownership. Those who did not have or did not work with children were encouraged to submit samples they found on the Internet that they found interesting, so everyone was able to contribute to the Padlet. The types of contributions ranged from video to audio to photos to text, and the students could choose to post anonymously or include their names in the post. The high participation rate and number of views suggest that the activity was inclusive and engaging for students.

Fostering Motivation and Confidence

In a fourth-year course which provided students with various understandings of pedagogical and content knowledge to successfully teach mathematics, students were encouraged to reflect in real time on the Padlet at the beginning of each tutorial. Padlet was used to help students articulate their expectations of the course and the instructor and to express their disciplinary understandings. The Padlet was formatted into columns and students could add their responses to the questions heading each column, for example, 'What are your expectations of this course?' and 'What are your expectations of me?' This reflective activity encouraged teachers to assess and reassess their motivations for studying (Getenet & Tualaulelei, 2023).

In the same course, students were presented with mathematics problems on Google Sheets. Each tab on the sheet had identical mathematics problems and small groups were encouraged to work together to solve them. For example, groups solved problems by posting pictures, generating graphs, and performing calculations from provided data. During these activities, students supported each other by clarifying the expectations of the activities and by explaining their assumptions underlying the solutions. Another way Google Sheets was used was for pre-service teachers to reflect on various numeration systems and their own school experiences. These problem-solving and reflection activities helped keep pre-service teachers motivated to work on mathematics which they commonly find challenging (Getenet & Tualaulelei, 2023).

Video-embedded quizzes also helped build pre-service teachers' confidence, particularly when they received affirmation that they had understood key concepts and ideas. Panopto quizzes did not allow mathematical symbols to be displayed, so they were most helpful for conceptual or theoretical knowledge checks. For example, a lecture video in a literacy course explained different theories of writing before pausing for a quiz question which asked, 'Which theory claims that children require fine motor skills and visual discrimination skills before they engage in writing?' Pre-service teachers could select from three answers: Developmental psychological, behavioural, or sociocultural (the answer is developmental psychological) and selecting the correct answer would play the video. We found that quizzes had to be carefully placed in the video (those placed at the end were commonly ignored) and that learners valued quizzes that were immediately relevant to video content. These brief knowledge checks helped pre-service teachers become more confident with the wide variety of teaching ideas they encountered while studying education.

Fostering Trust

Affective engagement was also promoted through Google Docs activities, where students were focused on collaborative problem-solving and task-relevant discussion. In a third-year early years course about intercultural communication, pre-service teachers were encouraged to do a group assignment on Google Slides. In early course iterations, this group assignment was left to each group to communicate about the group presentation, organise its creation, and execute it. However, it reached a point where more groups were malfunctioning rather than functioning, and this necessitated more guidance from the instructor. In an initial meeting with each group, the instructor discussed with the group members the assignment expectations as well as ideas for successful collaboration. A member of the group then set up a Google Slides presentation as a draft for the actual presentation and shared the link. Once everyone was accessing the presentation (visible through icons at the top of the screen), they worked together to create slides with tentative titles or sections for the presentation. When the group had a structure in place, the instructor answered any last questions and instructed the group members to stay online to delegate responsibility for each section of the presentation, including the duties of final formatting, proofreading, and referencing and to set deadlines. The instructor then left the meeting and the group continued collaborating through the document they had created.

Starting this group assignment with the instructors' guidance helped pre-service teachers get to know each other in a safe setting, and it helped establish a sense of trust. Online students often have few opportunities for synchronous interaction, so they may study whole courses without ever interacting in real-time with a peer. Video-conferencing software such as Zoom helps bridge the distance between online learners, and Google Slides, in this example, helped to corral the group work and communication into one platform. Moreover, its version-recording capabilities helped keep a record of each group member's contribution. This transparency is useful if group work breaks down at a later stage, as it can provide evidence of what each individual has contributed. These technologies helped to foster trust amongst individual group members and resulted in a far higher success rate for this assignment than previous ways of working.

Fostering Well-Being and Enjoyment

Using interactive technologies helped students enjoy the process of learning as this encouraged interaction with course content and with online peers. During small group problem-solving activities in a mathematics course, pre-service teachers were observed engaging in banter and laughing during conversations. They shared their background experiences and confirmed or challenged ideas with others. In highly collaborative groups, members actively sought to involve every person who was online and those who did not have their cameras on or who could not contribute by audio (perhaps due to background noise) contributed by writing in the chat.

For interactive technologies to foster enjoyment, learning activities need to be well set up and running smoothly. Online learners can become frustrated when technology is not working as it should or when instructions are unclear. As one of our students remarked, '[It is] important to allow for some instruction/ working out how to use the technology time whenever you use new technology for people who have not used them before'. This reinforces the need for instructors to know the digital capabilities of their learners and to step them through activities before asking groups to work independently.

Fostering Commitment to Learning

Video-embedded quizzes encouraged pre-service teachers to commit to learning by giving them a sense of achievement when they answered questions correctly. Quizzes highlighted areas that learners had mastered and those they had yet to master, contributing to a renewal of commitment to learning. Some quiz functions were not used in our courses, but they have the potential to foster pre-service teachers' commitment. It is possible, for example, to configure the quiz so that when a learner answers a question incorrectly, they are taken back to a relevant point of the video to rewatch and repeat the quiz. Instructors can also configure quizzes so that incorrect answers provide responsive feedback or additional resources to help learners understand the correct answers.

Across all courses, during small group work, students were observed engaging in small talk about their studies outside the course or life outside the university. These conversations typically happened before or after the designated learning task was attempted, and they often centred on upcoming assignments, the lecturer's teaching styles or expectations, incidents that occurred in other courses, complaints about the university, and so on. These conversations helped pre-service teachers manage their expectations about university study and empathise with other students. From this brief, but meaningful, interactions, pre-service teachers could put their study workloads into perspective and renew their commitment to learning.

Fostering Reflective Dispositions

In a fourth-year mathematics course which provides students with basic mathematical competencies for tertiary studies in bachelor degree programmes, Padlet was used to gather students' feedback and ideas about tutorial topics anonymously. Professional reflection is a core skill for many professions, including teaching. Through articulating beliefs, values, and attitudes in reflections, teachers connect these to academic literature or educational guiding documents to make sense of their practice. When used synchronously and anonymously, Padlet allowed teachers to practise reflecting and to observe others reflecting in a low-stake learning activity. This can promote reflective dispositions in pre-service teachers and help them confront the assumptions and biases they hold about teaching and learning.

Countering Negative Affect

While we have lauded the usefulness of interactive technologies for promoting positive affect, it is also worth considering their value for countering dimensions of negative affect such as disinterest, boredom, frustration, anxiety, and feeling excluded. Interactive technologies will not automatically address all these dimensions, but they offer a range of activities that can help students overcome temporary dips in negative affect (Audrin & Hascoët, 2024; Murdoch & Lim, 2022). For example, we have observed disinterested students who usually had their cameras off and microphones muted in tutorials become far more active with activities that used interactive technologies, perhaps because they felt an extra sense of responsibility to their online peers or because their contributions were more clearly visible. We have also observed students who entered tutorials with various levels of frustration and stress exhibiting relief after discussing their worries with online peers prior to group activities, highlighting the value of affective engagement for online learner success.

4.4 Summary

Affective engagement is often overlooked in favour of cognitive and behavioural engagement, mainly because those types of engagement are more readily measured and evaluated. However, this section has demonstrated that affective engagement can mediate the development of other types of engagement. When pre-service teachers positively affect their studies – that is, they feel motivated, enthusiastic, interested, and have a sense of joy and well-being – they have more emotional and mental resources to direct towards engaging cognitively and behaviourally as learners. On the other hand, pre-service teachers who experience negative affect – that is, frustration, anger, stress, anxiety, boredom, exclusion, and so on – will disengage from online learning more readily. Affective engagement is fundamental for online pre-service teachers because if they can experience the joy of learning, they will also gain insights into the value and potential of positive affect for their own future students. Moreover, as we have shown through the practice examples and explanations, the promotion of positive affect can enhance the behavioural and cognitive aspects of learning. The last part of this section shared ideas for using interactive technologies for this purpose. The next section explores other dimensions of engagement which we observed in our courses.

5 Other Types of Engagement

Section 5 focuses on forms of engagement beyond the three types previously addressed that are observable in online learning settings and offers practical examples of how interactive technologies enhance these forms of engagement. Specifically, the section focuses on social and collaborative engagement as pre-service teachers interact with their peers and teachers and start to build professional networks. It also examines the development, within these networks, of working practices that pre-service teachers will likely carry forward into their future careers. Finally, the section concludes with a summary of its key points.

5.1 Other Types of Engagement in Online Teacher Education

Although much of the literature related to online engagement incorporates the three key dimensions of cognitive, behavioural, and affective engagement, as discussed so far in this element (for example, Dewan et al., 2019; Fredricks et al., 2004), several other dimensions of learner engagement have been proposed in the literature. Pittaway's (2012) engagement framework conceptualised five dimensions of engagement: intellectual, social, academic, professional, and personal, suggesting that there are dimensions beyond the key three. Social engagement, for instance, is often recognised across studies (Bergdahl & Hietajärvi, 2022; Parsons & Taylor, 2011). In the online teacher education context, Redmond et al. (2018) presented five dimensions of engagement for teaching and learning: cognitive, behavioural, emotional, social, and collaborative. Notably, this framework distinguishes between social and collaborative engagement as distinct forms of engagement. However, other research suggests that collaboration is a learning method, with social engagement as a driving force behind collaborative learning (Aalto & Mustonen, 2022; Gokbel, 2020). In other words, collaboration may be seen not as a standalone type of engagement but rather as a tool for fostering collaborative learning through social engagement. Adding to this contention is the idea that collaborative engagement could be considered part of behavioural, cognitive, *and/or* emotional engagement (Bond et al., 2020). As research continues in student engagement, these grey areas of engagement will begin to find clarity, but for now, social and collaborative engagements are treated separately as per Redmond et al. (2018).

Social engagement plays a crucial role in enhancing student learning and integration within educational communities, as evidenced by various scholarly studies. Garrison et al. (2001) described social engagement as a form of social presence through which learners can project their identity and personal characteristics into the community of inquiry, thereby encouraging peer interaction. These social opportunities enable students to be exposed to a diversity of views, which in turn facilitates a deepening and extension of their own beliefs and perspectives, highlighting certain components of social connectedness (Luo et al., 2022; Waters & Gasson, 2006). Pittaway (2012) also noted the importance of social engagement for pre-service teachers in online environments, whereby learners are given the opportunity to get to know members of their classes, make friends in their classes, and engage in social activities inside and outside the classroom. It may involve the willingness of users to engage in an online forum and depend on the level of openness and safety they feel in interacting with other participants, and importantly, it involves cooperation and collaboration (Kim et al., 2015). Redmond et al. (2018) described social engagement in similar terms, adding that in an online environment, social interactions are often in the form of learners talking about themselves and their contexts, which may result in ongoing interactions through social media. Highlighting various published sources, Redmond et al. (2018) also described social engagement as social interactions, relational engagement, and social presence.

Related to social engagement, collaborative engagement extends the networks that students engage with, looking beyond the university context. According to Redmond et al. (2018, p. 194), 'Collaborative engagement is related to the development of different relationships and networks that support learning, including collaboration with peers, instructors, industry, and the educational institution.' It overlaps with social engagement, particularly when referring to activities carried out in online courses, but it also goes beyond this when it involves institutional and professional opportunities for collaboration. An example of professional opportunities for collaborative engagement is when pre-service teachers engage with the teaching profession through professional development together. An example of institutional opportunities might be service-learning activities, where pre-service teachers mentor homework or reading clubs in schools. These types of opportunities enrich the educational experience and help pre-service teachers understand the relevance and currency of what they are studying.

Enhancing social and collaborative engagement in online learning environments contributes to a range of positive educational outcomes for students. It helps pre-service teachers successfully transition into the online environment because it provides opportunities for students to develop working relationships with their online peers and collaborate in learning. It helps pre-service teachers become active participants, listeners, problem-solvers, and co-developers of common group goals, rules, and tasks (Garrison, 2017). In addition, evidence in the literature suggests that social and collaborative engagement may be crucial to students' satisfaction with online studies and positively influence learning outcomes (Grieve et al., 2016; Molinillo et al., 2018). A key benefit is for pre-service teachers to develop professional networks and ways of working within these networks that they may take with them into the future (Bergdahl & Hietajärvi, 2022; Downing et al., 2019; Zygouris-Coe, 2019), because teaching is a social and collaborative endeavour.

5.1.1 Indicators and Measures of Social and Collaborative Engagement

Various studies have identified multiple indicators and measures of social engagement. According to Waters and Gasson (2006), social engagement is a sustained learning process in which learners engage with repeated externalisation, translation, and internalisation cycles to develop their own and community understanding. From their perspective, social engagement denotes 'active commitment to the social facilitation and direction of the community learning process' (p. 5). Similarly, Bergdahl and Hietajärvi (2022) suggested that indicators of social engagement in learning include interaction, reflection, and collaborative learning activities. Bond and Bergdahl (2022) identified collaborating and interacting with teachers and peers, shared knowledge building, asking for help, and caring for others as indicators of social engagement. Similarly, Lu and Churchill (2012) identified interacting with others, sharing ideas, collaborating on learning tasks to co-construct knowledge, and feeling a sense of learning community as indicators of social engagement. Redmond et al. (2018) described social engagement in relation to students building social community, creating a sense of belonging, developing relationships with peers, and establishing trust. These studies collectively highlight the significance of interaction, collaborative learning, reflection, and the construction of a supportive learning community as central pillars of social engagement. For pre-service teachers, understanding these indicators – ranging from fostering interaction and collaboration to fostering a sense of belonging and mutual support among students – can equip them to create more inclusive, interactive, and engaging online learning experiences.

In both online and traditional teaching approaches, measurement of social engagement is based on students' involvement in academic activities, ability to establish and maintain relationships, the quality of social interactions with peers and teachers (Deng et al., 2020), social presence (Garrison, 2007), sociability, and connectedness (Kim et al., 2015). Social presence, sociability, and connectedness are often measured through self-report questionnaires, interviews, observational checklists, and teachers' informal observation of gestures and non-verbal features. Other studies, such as Hoi and Le Hang (2021), measured social engagement using four items, asking students about the quality of, and effort required to maintain, relationships with friends and teachers when they participate in online learning activities (for example, 'I share learning materials with online classmates'). In the context of teacher education, Getenet et al. (2022) and Getenet and Tualaulelei (2023) used questionnaires, data analytics, and observations to measure social engagement. However, a shift in online learning and technological advances is paving the way for automatic generation, collection, and measurement of engagement. Interactive technologies not only provide users with advantages such as openness, accessibility, and collaboration, but they also lead to the automatic generation of data to measure learners' engagement and outcomes (Caspari-Sadeghi, 2022; Deng et al., 2020; Getenet & Tualaulelei, 2023). Dewan et al. (2019) classified the existing methods of identifying and measuring social engagement into three main categories – automatic, semi-automatic, and manual – considering the methods' dependencies on learners' participation. Further, the methods in each category were divided into subcategories based on the types of data used, for example, audio, video, and learner log data. In particular, the 'computer vision-based methods' in the automatic category that used facial expressions were examined because they were nonintrusive and cost-effective when considering the hardware and software needed for capturing and analysing video data. This technology is promising for measuring social engagement in future online learning environments.

Collaborative engagement can be measured in similar ways to social engagement, using different indicators. In measuring what they called 'professional engagement', Pittaway and Moss (2014) drew upon data collected through the learning management system along with course-related correspondence and evaluations. Meyer (2014) described 'Enriching educational experiences' as those that included 'interactions with diverse others and participation with learning communities, service learning, internships, and research with faculty'. Meyer (2014) suggested that surveys used for traditional measures of university student engagement, such as Indiana University's *National Survey of Student Engagement*, could be modified for online learning contexts, particularly the engagement indicators for collaborative learning, discussions with diverse others, student–faculty interaction, quality of interactions in the campus environment, and a supportive campus environment. Redmond et al. (2018) proposed four illustrative indicators of collaborative engagement: learning with peers, interacting with faculty members, connecting to institutional opportunities, and developing professional networks. No suggestions are made for collecting data for these indicators but combined with insights from Pittaway and Moss (2014) and Meyer (2014), the use of a range of learning management system data analytics and student self-reports through surveys and course evaluations appears to be the best place to start.

5.2 Promoting Other Types of Engagement with Interactive Technologies

Technology-enhanced learning facilitates social engagement and has become attractive in higher education for promoting interaction (Gokbel, 2020). In addition, the way we work, collaborate, and communicate is ever-evolving with available communication and collaboration tools (for example, online collaborative spaces, Skype, social networking tools, and mobile devices) transforming online higher education and enabling students to interact and learn from a distance (Zygouris-Coe, 2019). According to Gokbel (2020), numerous emerging online tools for social interaction are available, including blogs/microblogs, wikis, discussion boards, voice-over-internet-protocol (VoIP) systems, web conferencing systems, real-time collaborative editing, shared spaces, text messaging, instant messaging, and chats that support online interactive learning. These technologies are used widely in online learning because higher education institutions are making extensive investments into online technologies.

A study by Molinillo et al. (2018) used web technologies (such as blogs, social networks, forums, and wikis) to improve higher education students' social engagement and facilitate their interactions. They found that the technologies encouraged communication among students, as well as between teachers and students, by providing a more continuous, asynchronous interaction and counteracting feelings of isolation that some students experienced. They argued that the technologies allowed students to actively create and share content, interact, collaborate, and generate knowledge, leading to greater student satisfaction with the learning experience. The social engagement promoted a sense of community that motivated learners to develop their learning in collaboration with their peers (Cho et al., 2015). Molinillo et al. (2018) designed a range of learning activities to use social media technologies to improve student social engagement as summarised in Table 8.

Table 8 Social-web-based tools and associated learning activities[a]

Tool	Learning activities
Blog	The blog enabled students to track their progress by comparing their reflections over the semester, engaging in critical exchanges with peers and external blog users, and sharing updates about the case study company and its industry.
Social network	Social networks enabled student interaction via various communication methods, enhancing analytical and critical thinking by exposing students' thoughts to a wide audience. By encouraging feedback and discussion, these platforms fostered a familiar, collaborative environment that improved engagement and learning in the case study.
File storage and sharing	Students leveraged a free platform for document sharing, streamlining collaboration and document access for their case study. This enabled organised, remote collaboration and safeguarded work through backup and recovery features, emphasising the importance of teamwork and engagement.

Table 8 (cont.)

Tool	Learning activities
Forum	The platform enhanced collaboration by enabling asynchronous discussions, knowledge sharing, and task coordination, deepening material comprehension. It also supported a second forum for news, announcements, and teacher-student communication, fostering engagement and query resolution.
Communication system	Skype enabled real-time voice and video discussions among group members, enhancing collaboration through frequent idea exchanges and immediate decision-making. Due to the quick pace, pre-meeting preparation was essential. It was used extensively for regular meetings and, crucially, for final presentations and case study discussions, emphasising its role in social engagement and teamwork.
Wiki	Through a wiki, students collaborated on case analysis and problem-solving, continually updating and refining content to develop informed solutions based on course knowledge.

[a] Molinillo et al., 2018, p. 46

Understanding the importance of interactive technologies for improving social and collaborative engagement is crucial for pre-service teachers as they prepare for the evolving educational and technological landscape. The ability to effectively utilise tools like blogs, social networks, forums, Skype, and wikis enhances participants' social presence within a course and promotes active learning and collaboration among learners. By integrating these technologies into their teaching strategies, pre-service teachers can better engage students from diverse backgrounds, thereby improving collaborative learning outcomes and preparing them for the realities of the digital world.

5.3 Practice Examples and Explanations of Impact

This section presents examples and explanations of how interactive technologies have been successfully implemented in teacher education courses.

Establishing trust: Google Slides was used mid-way through a first-year post-graduate literacy course to help group members establish trust with each other by collectively reviewing course readings. The whole class was divided into smaller break-out groups and each group was allocated a slide corresponding to a week of readings. The group task was to summarise the readings for the week on one side of the slide and, on the other side of the slide, to provide advice for others about how the readings could be used to support assignment tasks. Google Slides helped establish trustful working relationships from the outset because pre-service teachers negotiated their knowledge in real time, knowing also that their work would be shared with the whole cohort, including those who accessed the slides asynchronously.

Learning with peers: In a mathematics course, pre-service teachers created and solved problems and discussed how to teach the concept of place value through primary school problem-solving approaches using Google Docs. They discussed different problem-solving strategies, compared answers, corrected mistakes collectively, and finally discussed different strategies for teaching the concept. This interactive approach with peers and colleagues helped to solidify their understanding of place value and enhanced their ability to teach the concept in their future classrooms.

In a post-course survey, pre-service teachers reported various levels of agreement about using the technologies to facilitate their social and collaborative engagement in studying the online mathematics education course (see Table 9).

As shown in Table 9, the pre-service teachers valued almost equally the utility of Google Docs, Padlet, and Panopto quizzes for enhancing their social

Table 9 Pre-service teachers' agreement on social and collaborative engagement impacts of technologies[a]

Engagement	Indicators[b]	Google Docs	Padlet	Panopto quiz
Social	Create sense of belonging	3.25	3.25	3.25
	Develop relationships with others	3.33	3.50	3.25
	Develop a sense of community among others	3.33	3.42	3.33
Collaborative	Engage with lecturers or tutors	3.50	3.67	3.33
	Connect to opportunities at the university	3.33	3.33	3.33
	Develop professional networks	3.00	3.25	3.25

[a] Getenet et al., 2022, p. 246
[b] Means ($N = 12$) on Likert scale: Strongly agree = 5, Agree = 4 Neutral = 3, Disagree = 2, Strongly disagree = 1

and collaborative engagement. In addition, although Padlet provided limited information on its analytics system, the number of posts, comments, and contributors were accessible, and there were 123 posts and 20 comments from 50 pre-service teachers, which indicated a high level of involvement. The recorded sessions, integrated with Padlet and Google Docs, were analysed, and the results are reported in Table 10.

Table 10 Observed frequencies of pre-service teachers' engagement in Padlet and Google Docs[a]

Engagement	Indicators	Google Docs (N)	Padlet (N)	Descriptive example
Social	Create sense of belonging	4	7	*Google Docs and Padlet:* Pre-service teachers managed activities while working in groups
	Develop relationships with others	8	4	*Google Docs*: Worked in pairs to answer questions *Padlet:* Commented on other pre-service teachers' responses
	Develop sense of community	8	6	*Google Docs and Padlet*: Worked in groups and created a community for further discussion
	Managing expectations	2	3	*Google Docs and Padlet*: Commented on the expectations of the activities
Collaborative	Engage with lecturers or tutors	10	8	Padlet: Answered questions for the lecturer in text form
	Connect to opportunities at the university	0	0	
	Develop professional networks	7	8	Google Docs and Padlet: Pre-service teachers shared links

[a] Getenet et al., 2022, p. 247

The observational data showed that both Padlet and Google Docs supported pre-service teachers' social engagement at different levels. When pre-service teachers were using Padlet, there were instances in which they engaged socially. However, Google Docs better supported pre-service teachers' social engagement. Examples of social engagement promoted by Google Docs included developing a sense of community with others ($N = 8$) and developing relationships with others ($N = 8$). The results showed that using technology in teaching can enhance pre-service teachers' engagement and improve their use of various technologies for their future profession. In addition, it showed the importance of teacher educators understanding and identifying the types of technologies most suitable to enhance each engagement dimension.

5.4 Summary

Studies suggest that integrating interactive technologies in online teacher education not only enriches pre-service teachers' learning experience but also equips them with the skills to foster engaging and collaborative online learning environments for their future students. Interactive technologies enhance online learning by improving social engagement among learners and educators and encouraging pre-service teachers to seek collaborative opportunities beyond the university. Tools, including blogs, social networks, forums, and real-time communication platforms, encourage interaction, community building, and collaborative learning. These, in turn, help pre-service teachers overcome isolation, improve their student satisfaction, and develop critical interpersonal and communication skills. Using such technologies in teacher training programmes is key for preparing learners for an increasingly digital world.

6 Where to from Here?

Throughout this Element, we have examined online student engagement as a multidimensional construct that describes how pre-service teachers engage with online learning, and we have demonstrated that online student engagement plays an important role in developing future teachers who are critical, committed, and engaging. This section summarises what student engagement looked like for our online pre-service teachers in terms of behavioural engagement, cognitive engagement, affective engagement, and other types of engagement, highlighting the role of interactive technologies. We discuss the challenges we faced in using the interactive technologies described in the previous sections, and we make suggestions for how to mitigate these challenges. The closing section offers recommendations on how online initial teacher education can utilise interactive technologies to 'grow' teachers who can effectively engage their own students. As the coronavirus pandemic showed the world, the transition to online-only learning may be a sudden necessity in the future, or perhaps online learning will become the norm in teacher education. In either case, issues of online student engagement are better explored and understood beforehand rather than 'in the moment'.

6.1 Online Pre-Service Teachers' Experience of Student Engagement

Across the range of subjects that we teach such as mathematics in the primary years, intercultural education, early language development, and literacy, the interactive technologies we utilised offered students multiple opportunities to engage with course content. Google Docs and Padlet were used as central organising tools for small-group collaborative work or whole class activities, while video-embedded quizzes were used in lecture recordings to hold viewers' attention and offer immediate formative feedback. Throughout this Element, we have explained the specific dimensions of online student engagement we observed and experienced and have shown with practical examples what these could look like in the online teaching and learning environment. In the summary that follows, we outline ideas about how these specific dimensions of student engagement have implications for pre-service teachers as teacher graduates and, ultimately, as full-fledged professional teachers.

Cognitive (Section 2): It is a teacher's job to know the business of teaching, so pre-service teachers need to be cognitively engaged to develop a deep understanding of the teaching profession. When they invest significant time and energy into their learning, they develop their capacity for decision-making in relation to theories of teaching and learning and the ability to think critically about all aspects of their professional roles. In the online learning environment, much of the development of our pre-service teacher's professional identity came from their deep and sustained interactions with educational ideas. This pedagogical and content knowledge carries the expectation that pre-service teachers possess knowledge about how to transform curriculum and content knowledge into pedagogy (Mäkinen et al., 2018). At times, this knowledge involves the adoption of new terminology, new ways of thinking, and new theories and ideas about how learners learn and how teachers teach. Interactive technologies helped our students gain this knowledge collaborative reflection on the ideas they were learning about, problem-solving in real-time, and engaging with ideas in dialectical and dialogical ways. Through interacting with more skilled peers and with less skilled peers, pre-service teachers were able to learn from and teach others.

Behavioural (Section 3): As professionals, teachers are expected to develop positive dispositions for lifelong learning. Because professional learning and development is increasingly a mixture of face-to-face and online experiences, its success depends on behaviours such as taking the initiative to direct one's learning and sharing professional ideas through writing and presentations. Our pre-service teachers were encouraged to use interactive technologies to articulate their ideas in a professional manner for their peers, share ideas for how to find resources, follow online communication norms (manners, turn-taking, conflict management, and so on), organise and manage their time, and develop their technology skills. These are all behavioural dispositions and skills that teachers will use on the job, but they also ensure that pre-service teachers will graduate to become professionals who can manage and maintain continuing professional learning (Darling-Hammond et al., 2017). For pre-service teachers who are new to university, learning the 'rules of the game' for online study and study more broadly contributed to their success as learners who were 'first in family/community to attend university'. Behavioural engagement enhances cognitive engagement, but beyond this, relationality and interpersonal skills are also encouraged.

Affective (Section 4): Affect describes how pre-service teachers engage emotionally and attitudinally with initial teacher education. Affective engagement can help build a pre-service teacher's confidence and motivation towards online learning and support the development of their identity as a teacher. By using interactive technologies, our pre-service teachers were able to share their commitment to learning and share the joy of studying with others. Online chats, comments, and verbal discussions helped pre-service teachers share stories of stress, instances of humour, and celebrations of study achievements. These lighter moments of study interaction were no less valuable than other dimensions of engagement because they helped students understand that learning involves emotions and attitudes as much as brains and appropriate behaviours. In other words, education is as much a relational endeavour as it is an intellectual one. For students from backgrounds unfamiliar with university study, affective engagement helped contribute to their sense of belonging to our university and our courses. It also helped mitigate the negative aspects of affect. In small group activities, for example, it was difficult for students to remain disinterested when the other members of the group were actively working together. Similarly, a pre-service teacher who was bored could express themselves to a smaller group of peers without feeling judged. If they felt anxious or frustrated about their technology or other skills, they were able to seek help from peers rather than from faculty if that was their preference.

Other types of engagement (Section 5): Overlapping with the previous three dimensions of engagement were social and collaborative engagement. Social engagement facilitated cognitive, behavioural, and affective engagement by developing peer-to-peer and peer-to faculty relationships. The collaborations from social engagement helped the pre-service teachers co-operate to complete activities and develop trust with each other. Although we have labelled these as 'other' dimensions of engagement, those were sometimes where the benefits of interactive technologies were most evident. Pre-service teachers interacted with course content and with each other, thus enhancing the cognitive, behavioural, and affective benefits of studying online. Social and collaborative engagement also lifted the overall mood of online learning in that it disrupted the traditional mode of university teaching (usually directed from faculty staff to pre-service teachers) by distributing knowledge and leadership amongst those who were online. These engagement aspects also differentiated video-embedded quizzes from other, more collaborative interactive technologies, such as Google Docs and Padlet. Online study is notoriously an individual pursuit. Isolation and high expectations of self-motivation, along with irregular and asynchronous communication, were features of previous generations of online learning experiences. Interactive technologies helped our students feel less isolated, more motivated, and more connected with those leading and participating in their classes. In using interactive technologies to promote online student engagement, we encouraged pre-service teachers to form, and participate in a professional learning community, which we hoped would continue beyond the course.

6.2 Challenges to Using Interactive Technologies

Pre-service teachers come to online learning with a wide spectrum of technological knowledge and skills. At one extreme, we have taught pre-service teachers whose previous educational experiences occurred before computers and the Internet were used for teaching and learning. At the other extreme, we have worked with pre-service teachers who have taught *us* innovative and creative applications for technology. While the technologies we have discussed in this Element were easy to use for most of our classes, there were times when technological challenges took up precious class time. For example, when Google Docs settings were not properly configured, it was difficult for students

Engaging Online Pre-service Teachers

to complete their group tasks. Similarly, if we had not explained an activity clearly enough, it would not generate the value for learning we intended. We have found success by approaching the use of interactive technologies with the assumption that all pre-service teachers benefit from basic step-by-step guidance. This modelled explicit teaching and was inclusive of all students no matter their technological abilities. What follows are tips and advice for using the three interactive technologies discussed throughout this Element.

6.2.1 Padlet Instructor Tips

- Decide what you want to achieve with the activity, whether it will be used for problem-solving, reflections, or demonstrations. Link Padlet activities to course module content.
- Purposefully select the settings. Decide beforehand whether students can post anonymous comments, the order of comments, and so on.
- Prepare clear instructions. Include instructions for use on or near the Padlet.
- Decide to use Padlet either during live sessions or after a live session or both. This will inform the type of questions to include in the Padlet.
- Embed the Padlet in the LMS rather than linking out (this takes advantage of the dynamic updating interface). If not embedded, make the links available afterwards for asynchronous contributions.
- Moderate the posts to avoid inappropriate or irrelevant interactions.

What to avoid:

- Avoid having too many Padlets. Try to have no more than two to three Padlet activities. Students do not like too much information in too many places.
- Don't make the activity overcomplicated.
- Avoid accidentally deleting posts because students are unlikely to repost.
- Don't change the layout mid-activity as this confuses learners.

6.2.2 Google Docs Instructor Tips

- Carefully design the activities, set up the framework, and decide on the questions or activities to be used. Think carefully about what can be achieved using Google Docs. It works well for group work during live sessions.
- Clearly label group sections/spaces, make them logically organised and accessible, and instruct students on how to find their group's section/ space.

- Offer a brief orientation for students on how to use the software if they are working in groups. Students might delete or change important information which other students might need.
- Remember to check settings beforehand. Ensure that the Google Docs link is shareable or else students cannot get into the document.
- Plan sufficient time for students to work on problems but set a time limit on the activity to increase student focus.
- Ensure that everyone understands the activity before moving into breakout rooms. Demonstrate the activity to students using your own shared screen and remind students that one student in each group should share their screen. Also explain how you can be contacted for assistance.
- Move around the breakout rooms to monitor, assist, and engage students.
- Offer an opportunity for groups to share their work or to reflect on the activity.
- Make the links available afterwards for asynchronous contributions.

What to avoid:

- Do not stay in one breakout room or with one small group during this activity – move around so students can access you and so that groups can work independently of you.
- Over-complicated activities will lead to student confusion and disengagement so ensure the activity layout is easy to understand and that the activity is sufficiently scaffolded by references to what students have learned previously.
- If using Google Docs asynchronously, refer to the document in tutorials or in forums so students can see how the document is developing.
- Activities that require the use of the maths equation editor may not be successful as it is time-consuming for the students to use. Use alternative software that is easier to use for maths formulae and writing.

6.2.3 Video-Embedded Quizzes Instructor Tips

- Intentionally select your preferred quiz settings.
- Ensure that the quiz questions are relevant to the embedded video.
- Understand that quizzes at the end of videos tend to be ignored.
- Periodically check in the analytics that students are engaging with the quizzes.
- Ask students to give you feedback if any quiz questions are incorrect or confusing.
- Address any student misconceptions evident through the quiz results in tutorials or in the LMS.

What to avoid:

- Don't create too many quiz questions. Quizzes are often short and informal questioning activities.
- Take care with the wording of quiz questions. Plain and unambiguous language is best.

6.3 Growing Teachers Who Can Engage Their Students.

So far, we have discussed online student engagement as a means for promoting pre-service teachers' academic success, but this is only one part of a larger picture which extends beyond initial teacher education. Most higher education institutions aim for graduates to gain selected attributes or competencies, usually including digital literacy skills, which are seen increasingly as a necessity for the contemporary knowledge society. Using interactive technologies for learning gives pre-service teachers a convenient way to build up these digital literacy skills, and to explore, and experiment with, unfamiliar technologies and their possibilities. They can build up their digital literacy skills in a safe environment with peers without feeling the pressure of being examined or assessed. Pre-service teachers already learn about a wide range of technologies to participate in tutorials and assignment work. Using interactive technologies incidentally can supplement this knowledge and help teachers be prepared if, for example, another pandemic forces all education online.

There is also a growing need for teachers to build relationality into their pedagogy and practice. Increasing student diversity and the need for more inclusive classroom environments mean that today's teachers must put effort into the quality of their relationships with students through showing care and empathy (Nieto, 2017; Noddings, 2008). According to Kriewaldt (2015, p. 85), 'Relationality is the connection between the teacher and the learner that is mediated by each participant's identity and agency. Such connections can range from nurturing and ethical to dominating and damaging. This means that the social and affective dimensions of learning can be valuable for learners who, for instance, may not feel a sense of belonging at school or find the school a challenging environment for learning. With the growing diversity of students in the classroom and the noticeably less diverse teaching profession, relational pedagogies and practices need to be modelled and experienced in initial teacher education. Through interactive technologies, our pre-service teachers shared banter, humour, empathy, and other interactions which reinforced that teaching and learning are not just intellectual activities focused on results. They are also opportunities to connect meaningfully with others and to experience transformative learning which is connected to one's own sense of curiosity and development. Digital skills and relationality are two areas of development that will remain important for the foreseeable future. The former is often explicitly included in teacher standards and curriculum expectations, while the latter is often ignored or receives a light touch in initial teacher education (Kriewaldt, 2015). Our work has shown that these can be developed hand-in-hand to promote the development of teachers who are both technologically literate and relational. This helps pre-service teachers become 'good teachers' which, as mentioned in Section 1, the public views as those who have positive relationships with their students (Haas et al., 2023).

Of particular importance is the maintenance of relational, affective, and social aspects of teaching and learning. The current educational climate is characterised by the increasing instrumentalisation of education which means that teachers and teacher educators alike are being strongly persuaded to adopt technicist approaches to education. This is evident in the rise of standardised curricula and assessments and teaching standards that are said to represent 'quality'. These normalising documents move the focus from what is important in teaching and learning – the social and humane dimensions of education. Interactive technologies are a reminder that education is a socially mediated activity conducted in and for communities and that collaboration is far more effective than competition in achieving goals. Using interactive technologies is a way of humanising the online learning experience and developing teachers who can generate trust and promote feelings of belonging. It is an act of resistance to forces that would measure teachers and learners by numbers, outcomes, productivity, performance, and rankings.

Furthermore, interactive technologies are important in pre-service education to enhance future teacher professionalism and teaching innovations. When teachers are confident with their digital tools, they can direct their cognitive resources towards other aspects of teaching. Tools fade into the background while ideas and innovation move to the front. When teachers understand the value of relational learning in online environments, they can enact relationality in their own classrooms, whether face-to-face, online, or at a distance. Teaching in the future will not be able to do without digital literacy or relationality. Without digital literacy, a teacher is ill-equipped for the modern world. Without relationality, the profession becomes merely technical rather than human.

When asked why they have chosen teaching as a profession, many pre-service teachers talk about being inspired by their own teachers at school and wanting to be a teacher who inspires their own students. When asked what they remember about their favourite teachers, their answers are rarely about how much a teacher knew or how qualified a teacher was – most times, their answers are about how much a teacher cared or how a teacher made learning fun. This has been our key motivation in understanding online student engagement. Our focus on interactive technologies in this Element is driven by how much we care about our students and how much we want them to care for their own students. We were driven by a desire for pre-service teachers to have such a great online learning experience that they want to emulate our style of teaching for their own students. We have both experienced, and admittedly taught, uninspiring online tutorials and we know how much better most tutorials are with interactive technologies because of the interactions and innovations that flow from activities centred around these. Whether a student would like to engage cognitively, behaviourally, affectively, or otherwise, interactive technologies allow all these dimensions to be experienced. Of course, this requires time and effort from faculty to learn to use new technologies, but these challenges are surmountable when they result in heightened engagement from pre-service teachers who will become the teachers of tomorrow and, some, the teacher educators of tomorrow.

6.4 Ideas for Future Research Directions

Across the several studies we have completed in this area, we suggest the following areas for future research:

Teacher educators' knowledge and use of interactive technologies: Pre-service teachers experience a wide range of exposure to interactive technologies, which is partly due to the knowledge and skills of their teacher educators in this area. Teacher educators who are less innovative or less interested in using interactive technologies for teaching and learning tend to use the technologies they are familiar with rather than exploring newer technologies as they become available. Teacher educators who are not supported with ongoing professional or technological support with interactive technologies are also less likely to try newer interactive technologies unless incentivised. Research is needed to understand what hinders and helps teacher educators' knowledge and capabilities for using interactive technologies and to understand what ongoing professional learning opportunities can lead to more extensive and effective uptake of interactive technologies.

In-depth understanding of online student engagement: There is no reason that the notion of online student engagement should remain opaque. Traditional studies of student engagement have provided a solid foundation for a better understanding of online student engagement. Furthermore, advanced technological tools and research methods enable the investigation of online student engagement through learning analytics, detailed logs, and assessment data. Future research might focus on a deeper understanding of online student engagement from the perspective of pre-service teachers, with implications for designing course activities to promote specific dimensions of student engagement. This would involve investigations into the impacts of educator presence and interactions between pre-service teachers.

Technology-specific studies: As new technologies emerge, more research is needed to help unpack the affordances of specific technologies and their impacts on online student engagement. The potential of virtual and augmented realities has not been fully explored, nor has the more recent phenomenon of artificial intelligence. Teacher educators can now set learning and assessment tasks that involve these technologies, however, their impact on online student engagement is not yet well understood. More research is needed to understand which technologies are most relevant and responsive for certain teaching disciplines.

Online student engagement across contexts: Research would also be useful to understand how pre-service teachers across diverse contexts, for instance, across disciplines or country/cultural contexts, engage with online initial teacher education. Which dimensions of engagement are valued when pre-service teachers are learning about teaching mathematics, literacy, science or other subjects? Which dimensions are important in different countries or cultural contexts? Which dimensions of engagement matter most to pre-service teachers with low socio-economic backgrounds, culturally diverse backgrounds, or disabilities? These and other questions deserve to be answered to ensure that 'online student engagement' does not become a catchphrase that means everything and nothing.

Online student engagement across the learning journey: Research assessing the long-term effects of interactive technologies on learning outcomes and material retention could be a fruitful area for future research. Much of our work has been over a few semesters with the longest period of study being eighteen months. Do experiences vary from level to level, that is, for students at the start of a degree programme compared with those at the end of their studies or those undertaking postgraduate studies? Longer-term studies, focused on pre-service teachers' journeys across a whole degree, would reveal how online student engagement develops from the first year of study until graduation. It might also capture reasons why students do not engage at all online and identify those who might be less likely to remain in their studies.

In conclusion, we return to our reasons for writing this Element. As teaching academics and researchers, we are interested in helping all online pre-service teachers experience positive and productive initial teacher education, much of which is being delivered online. This Element discussed several dimensions of online student engagement – cognitive, behavioural, affective, and others. We have argued throughout for a focus on developing pre-service teachers' digital skills and knowledge and building their capacity for relational pedagogies and practices. We have illustrated what this looked like in our own teaching contexts but do no doubt that other versions of these activities are happening in initial teacher education programmes across the globe. This Element is a call for teacher educators to share their practices and conduct a deeper dive into their rationale for incorporating specific technologies and activities into their teaching and learning. Ultimately, this body of research will benefit pre-service teachers and teacher education overall.

References

Aalto, E., & Mustonen, S. (2022). Designing knowledge construction in pre-service teachers' collaborative planning talk. *Linguistics and Education*, **69**, 1–12. https://doi.org/10.1016/j.linged.2022.101022.

Al Mamun, M. A., & Lawrie, G. (2023). pp. 1-31. *Smart Learning Environments*, **10**(1), 1–31. https://doi.org/10.1186/s40561-022-00221-x.

Alwafi, E. M., Downey, C., & Kinchin, G. (2020). Promoting pre-service teachers' engagement in an online professional learning community. *Journal of Professional Capital and Community*, **5**(2), 129–146. https://doi.org/10.1108/jpcc-10-2019-0027.

Anderson, T., & Shattuck, J. (2012). Design-based research: A decade of progress in education research? *Educational Researcher*, **41**(1), 16–25. https://doi.org/10.3102/0013189X11428813.

Anderson, B., & Simpson, M. (2004). Group and class contexts for learning and support online: Learning and affective support online in small group and class contexts. *The International Review of Research in Open and Distributed Learning*, **5**(3), 1–15. https://doi.org/10.19173/irrodl.v5i3.208.

Antonaci, A., Klemke, R., & Specht, M. (2019). The effects of gamification in online learning environments: A systematic literature review. *Informatics*, **6**(3), 1–22. https://doi.org/10.3390/informatics6030032.

Apple, M. W. (1995). *Education and power*. New York: Routledge.

Arif, F. K. M., Noah, J. B., Affendi, F. R., & Yunus, M. M. (2020). Paddle your way into writing: Integrating Padlet for ESL learners. *International Journal of Scientifed and Technology Research*, **9**(3), 5407–5410. www.ijstr.org/final-print/mar2020/Paddle-Your-Way-Into-Writing-Integrating-Padlet-For-Esl-Learners.pdf.

Attard, C., & Holmes, K. (2020). 'It gives you that sense of hope': An exploration of technology use to mediate student engagement with mathematics. *Heliyon*, **6**(1), 1–11. https://doi.org/10.1016/j.heliyon.2019.e02945.

Audrin, C., & Hascoët, M. (2024). Ode to joy: The impact of enjoyment on pre-service teacher persistence. *Teaching and Teacher Education*, **137**, 1–10. https://doi.org/10.1016/j.tate.2023.104406.

Australian Institute for Teaching and School Leadership. (2018). *Spotlight: The rise of online teacher education: What do we know?* www.aitsl.edu.au/docs/default-source/research-evidence/spotlight/ite-online.pdf.

Australian Institute for Teaching and School Leadership. (2023a). *Spotlight: Australia's teacher workforce today.* www.aitsl.edu.au/research/spotlights/australia-s-teacher-workforce-today.

Australian Institute for Teaching and School Leadership. (2023b). *Spotlight: Technological innovations in initial teacher education.* www.aitsl.edu.au/research/spotlights/technological-innovations-in-initial-teacher-education.

Bawa, P. (2016). Retention in online courses. *Sage Open*, **6**(1), 1–11. https://doi.org/10.1177/2158244015621777.

Bedenlier, S., Bond, M., Buntins, K., Zawacki-Richter, O., & Kerres, M. (2020). Facilitating student engagement through educational technology in higher education: A systematic review in the field of arts and humanities. *Australasian Journal of Educational Technology*, **36**(4), 126–150. https://doi.org/10.14742/ajet.5477.

Bergdahl, N., & Hietajärvi, L. (2022). Social engagement in distance-, remote-, and hybrid learning. *Journal of Online Learning Research*, **8**(3), 315–342. www.learntechlib.org/p/221444/.

Bolliger, D. U., & Martin, F. (2018). Instructor and student perceptions of online student engagement strategies. *Distance Education*, **39**(4), 568–583. https://doi.org/10.1080/01587919.2018.1520041.

Bond, M., & Bergdahl, N. (2022). Student engagement in open, distance, and digital education. In V. I. Marin & L. Castañeda (Eds.), *Handbook of open, distance and digital education*. Singapore: Springer Nature, pp. 1–16. https://doi.org/10.1007/978-981-19-0351-9_79-1.

Bond, M., Buntins, K., Bedenlier, S., Zawacki-Richter, O., & Kerres, M. (2020). Mapping research in student engagement and educational technology in higher education: A systematic evidence map. *International Journal of Educational Technology in Higher Education*, **17**(2), 1–30. https://doi.org/10.1186/s41239-019-0176-8.

Bostock, W. (1999). The global corporatisation of universities: Causes and consequences. *AntePodium*. https://hdl.handle.net/102.100.100/492466.

Bote-Lorenzo, M. L., & Gómez-Sánchez, E. (2017). Predicting the decrease of engagement indicators in a MOOC. In *Proceedings of the Seventh International Learning Analytics & Knowledge Conference*, pp. 143–147. https://doi.org/10.1145/3027385.3027387.

Bourdieu, P. (1998). *The state nobility: Elite schools in the field of power* (L. C. Clough, Trans.). New York: Polity Press.

Bourdieu, P., & Passeron, J.-C. (1990). *Reproduction in education, society and culture* (R. Nice, Trans.). Thousand Oaks, CA: SAGE.

Breslow, L., D. E. Pritchard, DeBoer, J. et al. (2013). Studying learning in the worldwide classroom: Research into edX's first MOOC. *Research and*

Practice in Assessment, **8**, 13–25. www.rpajournal.com/dev/wp-content/uploads/2013/05/SF2.pdf.

Brigham, T. J. (2014). Taking advantage of Google's web-based applications and services. *Medical Reference Services Quarterly*, **33**(2), 202–210. https://doi.org/10.1080/02763869.2014.897521.

Burke, K., Fanshawe, M., & Tualaulelei, E. (2022). We can't always measure what matters: Revealing opportunities to enhance online student engagement through pedagogical care. *Journal of Further and Higher Education*, **46**(3), 287–300. https://doi.org/10.1080/0309877X.2021.1909712.

Burns, M. (2023). *Distance education for teacher training: Modes, models, and methods*, 2nd ed., Washington, DC: Education Development Center. www.edc.org/distance-education-teacher-training-modes-models-and-methods.

Cakir, H. (2013). Use of blogs in pre-service teacher education to improve student engagement. *Computers & Education*, **68**, 244–252. https://doi.org/10.1016/j.compedu.2013.05.013.

Carrillo, C., & Flores, M. A. (2020). COVID-19 and teacher education: A literature review of online teaching and learning practices. *European Journal of Teacher Education*, **43**(4), 466–487. https://doi.org/10.1080/02619768.2020.1821184.

Caspari-Sadeghi, S. (2022). Applying learning analytics in online environments: Measuring learners' engagement unobtrusively. *Frontiers in Education*, **7**, 1–6. https://doi.org/10.3389/feduc.2022.840947.

Castro, A. J. (2010). Themes in the research on preservice teachers' views of cultural diversity: Implications for researching millennial preservice teachers. *Educational Researcher*, **39**(3), 198–210. https://doi.org/10.3102/0013189x10363819.

Chan, S., Maneewan, S., & Koul, R. (2021). Teacher educators' teaching styles: Relation with learning motivation and academic engagement in pre-service teachers. *Teaching in Higher Education*, **28**(8), 2044–2065. https://doi.org/10.1080/13562517.2021.1947226.

Chi, M. T. H. (2021). Translating a theory of active learning: An attempt to close the research-practice gap in education. *Topics in Cognitive Science*, **13**(3), 441–463. https://doi.org/10.1111/tops.12539.

Chigeza, P., & Halbert, K. (2014). Navigating e-learning and blended learning for pre-service teachers: Redesigning for engagement, access and efficiency. *Australian Journal of Teacher Education*, **39**(11), 133–146. https://doi.org/10.14221/ajte.2014v39n11.8.

Cho, M.-H., Cheon, J., & Lim, S. (2021). Preservice teachers' motivation profiles, self-regulation, and affective outcomes in online learning. *Distance Education*, **42**(1), 37–54. https://doi.org/10.1080/01587919.2020.1869528.

Cho, Y. H., Yim, S. Y., & Paik, S. (2015). Physical and social presence in 3D virtual role-play for pre-service teachers. *The Internet and Higher Education*, **25**, 70–77. https://doi.org/10.1016/j.iheduc.2015.01.002.

Chong, E. K. (2018). Developments and challenges of civic education in Hong Kong SAR, China (1997–2017). *The Journal of Social Studies Education in Asia*, **7**, 47–63. http://jerass.com/jssea/wp-content/uploads/2019/10/JSSEA_Vol7_47-63.pdf.

Chung, J.-Y., & Jeong, S.-H. (2024). Korean pre-service teachers' experiences of creating an online teaching portfolio in the teacher preparation course. *Journal of Educational and Social Research*, **14**(2), 1–10. https://doi.org/10.36941/jesr-2024-0021.

Clark, S. K., & Byrnes, D. (2015). What millennial preservice teachers want to learn in their training. *Journal of Early Childhood Teacher Education*, **36**(4), 379–395. https://doi.org/10.1080/10901027.2015.1100148.

Corcoran, R. P., & Tormey, R. (2012). How emotionally intelligent are pre-service teachers? *Teaching and Teacher Education*, **28**(5), 750–759. https://doi.org/10.1016/j.tate.2012.02.007.

Cummins, S., Beresford, A. R., & Rice, A. (2016). Investigating engagement with in-video quiz questions in a programming course. *IEEE Transactions on Learning Technologies*, **9**(1), 57–66. https://doi.org/10.1109/tlt.2015.2444374.

Dacko, A., Leung, L., Mohad, M., & Vandeloo, M. (2015). Making it personal: Understanding the online learning experience to enable design of an inclusive, integrated e-learning solution for students. *eLearning Papers*, **42**(1), 1–14. http://openresearch.ocadu.ca/id/eprint/1244/.

Daher, W., Sabbah, K., & Abuzant, M. (2021). Affective engagement of higher education students in an online course. *Emerging Science Journal*, **5**(4), 545–558. https://doi.org/10.28991/esj-2021-01296.

Darling-Aduana, J. (2019). Behavioral engagement shifts among at-risk high school students enrolled in online courses. *AERA Open*, **5**(4), 1–19. https://doi.org/10.1177/2332858419887736.

Darling-Hammond, L., Hyler, M. E., & Gardner, M. (2017). *Effective teacher professional development*. Washington, DC: Learning Policy Institute. https://learningpolicyinstitute.org/sites/default/files/product-files/Effective_Teacher_Professional_Development_REPORT.pdf.

Deeley, S. J. (2018). Using technology to facilitate effective assessment for learning and feedback in higher education. *Assessment & Evaluation in Higher Education*, **43**(3), 439–448. https://doi.org/10.1080/02602938.2017.1356906

Delamarter, J., & Wiederholt, K. (2019). The affective vs. the academic: A quantitative study of pre-service teachers' expected impact on their future students. *Action in Teacher Education*, **42**(2), 137–148. https://doi.org/10.1080/01626620.2019.1649742.

Deng, R., Benckendorff, P., & Gannaway, D. (2020). Learner engagement in MOOCs: Scale development and validation. *British Journal of Educational Technology*, **51**(1), 245–262. https://doi.org/10.1111/bjet.12810.

Deni, A. R. M., & Zainal, Z. I. (2018). Padlet as an educational tool: Pedagogical considerations and lessons learnt. In M. Nakayama & F. Lou (Eds.), *Proceedings of the 10th International Conference on Education Technology and Computers*, Association for Computing Machinery, New York, NY, USA, pp. 156–162. https://doi.org/10.1145/3290511.3290512.

Dewan, M. A. A., Murshed, M., & Lin, F. (2019). Engagement detection in online learning: A review. *Smart Learning Environments*, **6**(1), 1–20. https://doi.org/10.1186/s40561-018-0080-z.

DeWitt, D., Alias, N., Ibrahim, Z., Shing, N. K., & Rashid, S. M. M. (2015). Design of a learning module for the Deaf in a higher education institution using Padlet. *Procedia – Social and Behavioral Sciences*, **176**, 220–226. https://doi.org/10.1016/j.sbspro.2015.01.464.

Dianati, S., Nguyen, M., Dao, P., Iwashita, N., & Vasquez, C. (2020). Student perceptions of technological tools for flipped instruction: The case of Padlet, Kahoot! and Cirrus. *Journal of University Teaching and Learning Practice*, **17**(5), 4, 1–16. https://doi.org/10.53761/1.17.5.4.

Dixson, M. D. (2015). Measuring student engagement in the online course: The Online Student Engagement scale (OSE). *Online Learning*, **19**(4), 1–15. https://doi.org/10.24059/olj.v19i4.561.

Donnison, S. (2009). Discourses in conflict: The relationship between Gen Y pre-service teachers, digital technologies and lifelong learning. *Australian Journal of Educational Technology*, **25**(3), 336–350. https://doi.org/10.14742/ajet.1138.

Dougiamas, M. (2025). *Pedagogy*. 8 March. https://docs.moodle.org/405/en/Pedagogy.

Downing, J., Dyment, J., & Stone, C. (2019). Online Initial Teacher Education in Australia: Affordances for Pedagogy, Practice and Outcomes. *Australian Journal of Teacher Education*, **44**(5), 57–79. https://doi.org/10.14221/ajte.2018v44n5.4.

Dunn, T. J., & Kennedy, M. (2019). Technology enhanced learning in higher education; motivations, engagement and academic achievement. *Computers & Education*, **137**, 104–113. https://doi.org/10.1016/j.compedu.2019.04.004.

Dyment, J. E., & Downing, J. J. (2019). Online initial teacher education: A systematic review of the literature. *Asia-Pacific Journal of Teacher Education*, **48**(3), 316–333. https://doi.org/10.1080/1359866x.2019.1631254.

Education Services Australia. (2021). Shaping Our Future: A ten-year strategy to ensure a sustainable, high-quality children's education and care workforce 2022–2031. www.acecqa.gov.au/sites/default/files/2021-10/ShapingOurFutureChildrensEducationandCareNationalWorkforceStrategy-September2021.pdf.

Ellis, D. (2015). Using Padlet to increase student engagement in lectures. In A. Jefferies & M. Cubric (Eds.), *14th European Conference on e-Learning: ECEl2015*. ECEL – European Conference on e-Learning. pp. 195–198. https://core.ac.uk/reader/228140577.

Ellis, R. A., & Bliuc, A.-M. (2019). Exploring new elements of the student approaches to learning framework: The role of online learning technologies in student learning. *Active Learning in Higher Education*, **20** (1), 11–24. https://doi.org/10.1177/1469787417721384.

Ferrer, J., Ringer, A., Saville, K., Parris, M. A., & Kashi, K. (2022). Students' motivation and engagement in higher education: The importance of attitude to online learning. *Higher Education*, **83**(2), 317–338. https://doi.org/10.1007/s10734-020-00657-5.

Fletcher, T., Ní Chróinín, D., & O'Sullivan, M. (2018). Developing deep understanding of teacher education practice through accessing and responding to pre-service teacher engagement with their learning. *Professional Development in Education*, **45**(5), 832–847. https://doi.org/10.1080/19415257.2018.1550099.

Fredricks, J. A., Blumenfeld, P. C., & Paris, A. H. (2004). School engagement: Potential of the concept, state of the evidence. *Review of Educational Research*, **74**(1), 59–109. https://doi.org/10.3102/00346543074001059.

Gameil, A. A., & Al-Abdullatif, A. M. (2023). Using digital learning platforms to enhance the instructional design competencies and learning engagement of preservice teachers. *Education Sciences*, **13**(4), 1–15. https://doi.org/10.3390/educsci13040334.

Garrison, D. R. (2007). Online community of inquiry review: Social, cognitive, and teaching presence issues. *Journal of Asynchronous Learning Networks*, **11**(1), 61–72. https://files.eric.ed.gov/fulltext/EJ842688.pdf.

Garrison, D. R. (2017). *E-learning in the 21st century: A framework for research and practice*. 3rd ed., New York: Routledge.

Garrison, D. R., Anderson, T., & Archer, W. (2001). Critical thinking, cognitive presence, and computer conferencing in distance education. *American Journal of Distance Education*, **15**(1), 7–23. https://doi.org/10.1080/08923640109527071.

Geri, N., Winer, A., & Zaks, B. (2017). Challenging the six-minute myth of online video lectures: Can interactivity expand the attention span of learners? *Online Journal of Applied Knowledge Management*, **5**(1), 101–111. https://doi.org/10.36965/ojakm.2017.5(1)101-111.

Getenet, S., & Tualaulelei, E. (2023). Using interactive technologies to enhance student engagement in higher education online learning. *Journal of Digital Learning in Teacher Education*, **39**(4), 220–234. https://doi.org/10.1080/21532974.2023.2244597.

Getenet, S., Worsley, S., Tualaulelei, E., & Pillay, Y. (2022). The role of technologies to enhance pre-service teachers' engagement in an online mathematics education course. In N. Fitzallen, C. Murphy, V. Hatisaru, & N. Maher (Eds.), *Mathematical confluences and journeys (Proceedings of the 44th Annual Conference of the Mathematics Education Research Group of Australasia)*, pp. 241–249. MERGA. https://merga.net.au/publications/annual-conference-proceedings/2022-conference-proceedings/.

Gill-Simmen, L. (2021). Using Padlet in instructional design to promote cognitive engagement: A case study of undergraduate marketing students. *Journal of Learning Development in Higher Education*, **20**, 1–14. https://doi.org/10.47408/jldhe.vi20.575.

Goepel, J. (2012). Upholding public trust: An examination of teacher professionalism and the use of Teachers' Standards in England. *Teacher Development*, **16**(4), 489–505. https://doi.org/10.1080/13664530.2012.729784.

Gokbel, E. N. (2020). Online collaborative learning in pre-service teacher education: A literature review. In E. Alqurashi (Ed.), *Handbook of research on fostering student engagement with instructional technology in higher education*. Hershey, PA: IGI Global, pp. 288–304.

Goode, E., Nieuwoudt, J., & Roche, T. (2022). Does online engagement matter? The impact of interactive learning modules and synchronous class attendance on student achievement in an immersive delivery model. *Australasian Journal of Educational Technology*, **38**(4), 76–94. https://doi.org/10.14742/ajet.7929.

Gregory, M. S.-J., & Lodge, J. M. (2015). Academic workload: The silent barrier to the implementation of technology-enhanced learning strategies in higher education. *Distance Education*, **36**(2), 210–230. https://doi.org/10.1080/01587919.2015.1055056.

Grieve, R., Padgett, C. R., & Moffitt, R. L. (2016). Assignments 2.0: The role of social presence and computer attitudes in student preferences for online versus offline marking. *The Internet and Higher Education*, **28**, 8–16. https://doi.org/10.1016/j.iheduc.2015.08.002.

Guo, W., Chen, Y., Lei, J., & Wen, Y. (2014). The effects of facilitating feedback on online learners' cognitive engagement: Evidence from the asynchronous online discussion. *Education Sciences*, **4**(2), 193–208. https://doi.org/10.3390/educsci4020193.

Haas, E., Fischman, G., & Pivovarova, M. (2023). Public beliefs about good teaching. *Research in Education*, **121**(1), 93–121. https://doi.org/10.1177/00345237231207717.

Hafour, M. F., & Alwaleedi, M. (2022). Students' emotional and behavioral engagement: Cloud-based Collaborative writing and learning analytics. *Computer Assisted Language Learning*, **23**(1), 374–400. https://callej.org/index.php/journal/article/view/385.

Hamsher, S., & Dieterich, C. A. (2017). Creating a positive atmosphere in online courses: Student ratings of affective variables in teacher education courses. *International Journal of Instructional Technology and Distance Learning*, **14**(7), 75–84. http://itdl.org/Journal/Jul_17/Jul17.pdf.

Harasim, L. (2000). Shift happens: Online education as a new paradigm in learning. *Internet and Higher Education*, **3**(1–2), 41–61. https://doi.org/10.1016/S1096-7516(00)00032-4.

Hawkey, K. (2006). Emotional intelligence and mentoring in pre-service teacher education: A literature review. *Mentoring & Tutoring: Partnership in Learning*, **14**(2), 137–147. https://doi.org/10.1080/13611260500493485.

Heffernan, A., Longmuir, F., Bright, D., & Kim, M. (2019). *Perceptions of teachers and teaching in Australia*. Monash University. www.monash.edu/perceptions-of-teaching/docs/Perceptions-of-Teachers-and-Teaching-in-Australia-report-Nov-2019.pdf.

Heggart, K., & Yoo, J. (2018). Getting the most from Google Classroom: A pedagogical framework for tertiary educators. *Australian Journal of Teacher Education*, **43**(3), 140–153. https://doi.org/10.14221/ajte.2018v43n3.9.

Henderson, M., Selwyn, N., & Aston, R. (2015). What works and why? Student perceptions of 'useful' digital technology in university teaching and learning. *Studies in Higher Education*, **42**(8), 1567–1579. https://doi.org/10.1080/03075079.2015.1007946.

Hew, K. F., Huang, B., Chu, K. W. S., & Chiu, D. K. W. (2016). Engaging Asian students through game mechanics: Findings from two experiment studies. *Computers & Education*, **92–93**, 221–236. https://doi.org/10.1016/j.compedu.2015.10.010.

Hoi, V. N., & Le Hang, H. (2021). The structure of student engagement in online learning: A bi-factor exploratory structural equation modelling approach. *Journal of Computer Assisted Learning*, **37**(4), 1141–1153. https://doi.org/10.1111/jcal.12551.

Holzberger, D., Maurer, C., Kunina-Habenicht, O., & Kunter, M. (2021). Ready to teach? A profile analysis of cognitive and motivational-affective teacher characteristics at the end of pre-service teacher education and the long-term effects on occupational well-being. *Teaching and Teacher Education*, **100**, 1–14. https://doi.org/10.1016/j.tate.2021.103285.

Hu, M., & Li, H. (2017). Student engagement in online learning: A review. In F. L. Wang, O. Au, K. K. Ng, J. Shang, & R. Kwan (Eds.), *Proceedings of the 2017 International Symposium on Educational Technology (ISET)*, pp. 39–43. https://doi.org/10.1109/iset.2017.17.

Hurlbut, A. R. (2018). Online vs. traditional learning in teacher education: A comparison of student progress. *American Journal of Distance Education*, **32**(4), 248–266. https://doi.org/10.1080/08923647.2018.1509265.

Jones, E. P., Wahlquist, A. E., Hortman, M., & Wisniewski, C. S. (2021). Motivating students to engage in preparation for flipped classrooms by using embedded quizzes in pre-class videos. *Innovations in Pharmacy*, **12**(1), 6. https://doi.org/10.24926/iip.v12i1.3353.

Jordan, K. (2014). Initial trends in enrolment and completion of massive open online courses. *The International Review of Research in Open and Distributed Learning*, **15**(1), 133–160. https://doi.org/10.19173/irrodl.v15i1.1651.

Kabilan, M. K. (2016). Using Facebook as an e-portfolio in enhancing pre-service teachers' professional development. *Australasian Journal of Educational Technology*, **32**(1), 19–31. https://doi.org/10.14742/ajet.2052.

Kahu, E. R. (2011). Framing student engagement in higher education. *Studies in Higher Education*, **38**(5), 758–773. https://doi.org/10.1080/03075079.2011.598505.

Kahu, E. R., & Nelson, K. (2017). Student engagement in the educational interface: Understanding the mechanisms of student success. *Higher Education Research & Development*, **37**(1), 58–71. https://doi.org/10.1080/07294360.2017.1344197.

Keller, M. M., Hoy, A. W., Goetz, T., & Frenzel, A. C. (2016). Teacher enthusiasm: Reviewing and redefining a complex construct. *Educational Psychology Review*, **28**, 743–769. https://doi.org/10.1007/s10648-015-9354-y.

Kenney, J., & Fisher, M. (2017). Investigating the impact of embedded questions in online presentations in a hybrid undergraduate educational psychology course. In J. P. Johnston (Ed.), *Proceedings of EdMedia 2017*. Waynesville, NC: Association for the Advancement of Computing in Education (AACE), pp. 850–853. www.learntechlib.org/primary/p/178394/.

Kim, Y., Glassman, M., & Williams, M. S. (2015). Connecting agents: Engagement and motivation in online collaboration. *Computers in Human Behavior*, **49**, 333–342. https://doi.org/10.1016/j.chb.2015.03.015.

Kimbrel, L. A., & Gantner, M. W. (2021). Student perceptions of instructor made videos with quizzes in an asynchronous online course. *International*

Journal of Educational Leadership Preparation, **16**(1), 24–44. https://files.eric.ed.gov/fulltext/EJ1313136.pdf.

Kordrostami, M., & Seitz, V. (2021). Faculty online competence and student affective engagement in online learning. *Marketing Education Review*, **32**(3), 240–254. https://doi.org/10.1080/10528008.2021.1965891.

Kovacs, G. (2016). Effects of in-video quizzes on MOOC lecture viewing. In J. Haywood (Ed.), *Proceedings of the Third (2016) ACM Conference on Learning @ Scale*. New York: Association for Computing Machinery, pp. 31–40. https://doi.org/10.1145/2876034.2876041.

Krause, K. L., & Coates, H. (2008). Students' engagement in first-year university. *Assessment & Evaluation in Higher Education*, **33**(5), 493–505. https://doi.org/10.1080/02602930701698892.

Kriewaldt, J. A. (2015). Strengthening learners' perspectives in professional standards to restore relationality as central to teaching. *Australian Journal of Teacher Education*, **40**(8), 83–98. https://doi.org/10.14221/ajte.2015v40n8.5.

Kuh, G. D. (2003). What we're learning about student engagement from NSSE: Benchmarks for effective educational practices. *Change: The Magazine of Higher Learning*, **35**(2), 24–32. https://doi.org/10.1080/00091380309604090.

Lacher, L. L., Jiang, A., Zhang, Y., & Lewis, M. C. (2018). Including coding questions in video quizzes for a flipped CS1. In T. Barnes & D. Garcia (Eds.), *Proceedings of the 49th ACM Technical Symposium on Computer Science Education*. New York: Association for Computing Machinery, pp. 574–579. https://doi.org/10.1145/3159450.3159504.

Lee, Y.-J., Davis, R., & Li, Y. (2022). Implementing synchronous online flipped learning for pre-service teachers during COVID-19. *European Journal of Educational Research*, **11**(2), 653–661. https://doi.org/10.12973/eu-jer.11.2.653.

Lee, Y., & Martin, K. I. (2019). The flipped classroom in ESL teacher education: An example from CALL. *Education and Information Technologies*, **25**(4), 2605–2633. https://doi.org/10.1007/s10639-019-10082-6.

Lei, M., Clemente, I. M., & Hu, Y. (2019). Student in the shell: The robotic body and student engagement. *Computers & Education*, **130**, 59–80. https://doi.org/10.1016/j.compedu.2018.11.008.

Li, L.-Y., & Tsai, C.-C. (2017). Accessing online learning material: Quantitative behavior patterns and their effects on motivation and learning performance. *Computers & Education*, **114**, 286–297. https://doi.org/10.1016/j.compedu.2017.07.007.

Li, S., Yu, C., Hu, J., & Zhong, Y. (2016). Exploring the effect of behavioral engagement on learning achievement in online learning environment: Learning analytics of non-degree online learning data. In C.-K. Chang, G.-J. Hwang, L. Chen et al. (Eds.), *Proceedings of the 2016 International Conference on*

Educational Innovation through Technology (EITT). New York: IEEE, pp. 246–250. https://doi.org/10.1109/eitt.2016.56.

Licorish, S. A., Owen, H. E., Daniel, B., & George, J. L. (2018). Students' perception of Kahoot!'s influence on teaching and learning. *Research and Practice in Technology Enhanced Learning*, **13**, 1–23. https://doi.org/10.1186/s41039-018-0078-8.

Lingard, B. (2018). Reforming education: The spaces and places of education policy and learning. In E. Hultqvist, S. Lindblad, & T. S. Popkewitz (Eds.), *Critical analyses of educational reforms in an era of transnational governance*. Springer International, Cham, pp. 41–60. https://doi.org/10.1007/978-3-319-61971-2_3.

Lu, J., & Churchill, D. (2012). The effect of social interaction on learning engagement in a social networking environment. *Interactive Learning Environments*, **22**(4), 401–417. https://doi.org/10.1080/10494820.2012.680966.

Luo, N., Li, H., Zhao, L., Wu, Z., & Zhang, J. (2022). Promoting student engagement in online learning through harmonious classroom environment. *The Asia-Pacific Education Researcher*, **31**(5), 541–551. https://doi.org/10.1007/s40299-021-00606-5.

MacKenzie, L., & Ballard, K. (2015). Can using individual online interactive activities enhance exam results? *MERLOT Journal of Online Learning and Teaching*, **11**(2), 262–266. https://jolt.merlot.org/Vol11no2/Ballard_0615.pdf.

Mäkinen, M., Linden, J., Annala, J., & Wiseman, A. (2018). Millennial generation preservice teachers inspiring the design of teacher education. *European Journal of Teacher Education*, **41**(3), 343–359. https://doi.org/10.1080/02619768.2018.1448776.

Martin, F., Sun, T., Turk, M., & Ritzhaupt, A. (2021). A meta-analysis on the effects of synchronous online learning on cognitive and affective educational outcomes. *The International Review of Research in Open and Distributed Learning*, **22**(3), 205–242. https://doi.org/10.19173/irrodl.v22i3.5263.

McKay, J., & Marshall, P. (2001). The dual imperatives of action research. *Information Technology & People*, **14**(1), 46–59. https://doi.org/10.1108/09593840110384771.

McKnight, K., O'Malley, K., Ruzic, R. et al. (2016). Teaching in a digital age: How educators use technology to improve student learning. *Journal of Research on Technology in Education*, **48**(3), 194–211. https://doi.org/10.1080/15391523.2016.1175856.

Mehta, K. J., Miletich, I., & Detyna, M. (2021). Content-specific differences in Padlet perception for collaborative learning amongst undergraduate students.

References

Research in Learning Technology, 29, 1–19. https://doi.org/10.25304/rlt.v29.2551.

Meyer, K. A. (2014). Student engagement in online learning: What works and why. *ASHE Higher Education Report*, 40(6), 1–114. https://doi.org/10.1002/aehe.20018.

Mills, G. E. (2007). *Action research: A guide for the teacher researcher* (3rd ed.). Upper Saddle River, NJ: Pearson Merrill Prentice Hall.

Molinillo, S., Aguilar-Illescas, R., Anaya-Sánchez, R., & Vallespín-Arán, M. (2018). Exploring the impacts of interactions, social presence and emotional engagement on active collaborative learning in a social web-based environment. *Computers & Education*, 123, 41–52. https://doi.org/10.1016/j.compedu.2018.04.012.

Morabito, M. G. (1999). *Online distance education: Historical perspective and practical application*. PhD, American Coastline University. www.dissertation.com/m/books/1581120575.

Morris, J., & Chi, M. T. H. (2020). Improving teacher questioning in science using ICAP theory. *The Journal of Educational Research*, 113(1), 1–12. https://doi.org/10.1080/00220671.2019.1709401.

Morrquin, D., Challoo, L., & Green, M. (2019). Teachers' perceptions regarding the use of Google Classroom and Google Docs. In S. Carliner (Ed.), *Proceedings of the E-Learn 2019: World Conference on E-Learning*. New Orleans, LA: Association for the Advancement of Computing in Education (AACE), pp. 21–30. www.learntechlib.org/p/211059/.

Moss, T., & Pittaway, S. (2018). Expectations and engagement: Key touchpoints in online students' experiences of transition. In M. Campbell, J. Willems, C. Adachi et al. (Eds.), *Open oceans: Learning without borders (Proceedings of the Australasian Society for Computers in Learning in Tertiary Education*. Geelong: Australasian Society for Computers in Learning in Tertiary Education,) pp. 460–465. https://2018conference.ascilite.org/wp-content/uploads/2018/12/ASCILITE-2018-Proceedings-Final.pdf.

Muljana, P. S., & Luo, T. (2019). Factors contributing to student retention in online learning and recommended strategies for improvement: A systematic literature review. *Journal of Information Technology Education: Research*, 18, 19–57. https://doi.org/10.28945/4182.

Murdoch, Y. D., & Lim, H. (2022). Exploring Korean College of Education pre-service teacher persistence toward a teaching career: Quantitative analysis of reasons and factors for persisting. *Sage Open*, 12(4), 1–14. https://doi.org/10.1177/21582440221129249.

Neumann, K. L., & Kopcha, T. J. (2019). Using Google Docs for peer-then-teacher review on middle school students' writing. *Computers and Composition*, **54**, 1–16. https://doi.org/10.1016/j.compcom.2019.102524.

Nieto, S. (2017). Re-imagining multicultural education: New visions, new possibilities. *Multicultural Education Review*, **9**(1), 1–10. https://doi.org/10.1080/2005615X.2016.1276671.

Noble, D. F. (1998). Digital diploma mills: The automation of higher education. *Science as Culture*, **7**(3), 355–368. https://doi.org/10.1080/09505439809526510.

Noddings, N. (2008). Caring and moral education. In L. Nucci, T. Krettenauer, & D. Narvaez (Eds.), *Handbook of moral and character education*. New York: Routledge, pp. 161–174.

Oakley, G., Pegrum, M., & Johnston, S. (2013). Introducing e-portfolios to pre-service teachers as tools for reflection and growth: Lessons learnt. *Asia-Pacific Journal of Teacher Education*, **42**(1), 36–50. https://doi.org/10.1080/1359866x.2013.854860.

Oxford University Press. (2025). *Interactive*. In Oxford English Dictionary. 7 March. www.oed.com/dictionary/interactive_adj?tl=true.

Özbek, T., Wekerle, C., & Kollar, I. (2023). Fostering pre-service teachers' technology acceptance – does the type of engagement with tool-related information matter? *Education and Information Technologies*, **29**(5), 6139–6161. https://doi.org/10.1007/s10639-023-12047-2.

Pan, X. (2023). Online learning environments, learners' empowerment, and learning behavioral engagement: The mediating role of learning motivation. *Sage Open*, **13**(4), 1–16. https://doi.org/10.1177/21582440231205098.

Parsons, J., & Taylor, L. (2011). Improving student engagement. *Current Issues in Education*, **14**(1), 1–33. https://cie.asu.edu/ojs/index.php/cieatasu/article/view/745.

Pifarre, M. (2019). Using interactive technologies to promote a dialogic space for creating collaboratively: A study in secondary education. *Thinking Skills and Creativity*, **32**, 1–16. https://doi.org/10.1016/j.tsc.2019.01.004.

Pittaway, S. M. (2012). Student and staff engagement: Developing an engagement framework in a faculty of education. *Australian Journal of Teacher Education*, **37**(4), 37–45. https://doi.org/10.14221/ajte.2012v37n4.8.

Pittaway, S. M., & Moss, T. (2014). 'Initially, we were just names on a computer screen': Designing engagement in online teacher education. *Australian Journal of Teacher Education*, **39**(7), 140–156. https://doi.org/10.14221/ajte.2014v39n7.10.

Pool, J., & Laubscher, D. (2016). Design-based research: Is this a suitable methodology for short-term projects? *Educational Media International*, **53**(1), 42–52. https://doi.org/10.1080/09523987.2016.1189246.

Ranellucci, J., Robinson, K. A., Rosenberg, J. M. et al. (2021). Comparing the roles and correlates of emotions in class and during online video lectures in a flipped anatomy classroom. *Contemporary Educational Psychology*, **65**, 1–15. https://doi.org/10.1016/j.cedpsych.2021.101966.

Ravindran, B., Greene, B. A., & Debacker, T. K. (2005). Predicting preservice teachers' cognitive engagement with goals and epistemological beliefs. *The Journal of Educational Research*, **98**(4), 222–233. https://doi.org/10.3200/joer.98.4.222-233.

Redmond, P., Heffernan, A., Abawi, L., Brown, A., & Henderson, R. (2018). An online engagement framework for higher education. *Online Learning*, **22**(1), 183–204. https://doi.org/10.24059/olj.v22i1.1175.

Reeve, J., & Tseng, C.-M. (2011). Agency as a fourth aspect of students' engagement during learning activities. *Contemporary Educational Psychology*, **36**(4), 257–267. https://doi.org/10.1016/j.cedpsych.2011.05.002.

Rice, P., Beeson, P., & Blackmore-Wright, J. (2019). Evaluating the impact of a quiz question within an educational video. *TechTrends*, **63**(5), 522–532. https://doi.org/10.1007/s11528-019-00374-6.

Richardson, J. C., & Newby, T. (2018). The role of students' cognitive engagement in online learning. *American Journal of Distance Education*, **20**(1), 23–37. https://doi.org/10.1207/s15389286ajde2001_3.

Saini, C., & Abraham, J. (2019). Implementing Facebook-based instructional approach in pre-service teacher education: An empirical investigation *Computers & Education*, **128**, 243–255. https://doi.org/10.1016/j.compedu.2018.09.025.

Schindler, L. A., Burkholder, G. J., Morad, O. A., & Marsh, C. (2017). Computer-based technology and student engagement: A critical review of the literature. *International Journal of Educational Technology in Higher Education*, **14**, 1–28. https://doi.org/10.1186/s41239-017-0063-0.

Schnackenberg, H. L. (2019). Are we part of the problem?: Teacher preparation programs, educational technology, and the mis-education of future teachers. In H. L. Schnackenberg & C. Johnson (Eds.), *Preparing the higher education space for Gen Z*. Hershey, PA: IGI Global, pp. 110–123.

Serrano, D. R., Dea-Ayuela, M. A., Gonzalez-Burgos, E., Serrano-Gil, A., & Lalatsa, A. (2019). Technology-enhanced learning in higher education: How to enhance student engagement through blended learning. *European Journal of Education*, **54**(2), 273–286. https://doi.org/10.1111/ejed.12330.

References

Shaw, N. (2023). Pre-service teachers as researchers of educational practices: Effects on students' narration of their learner autobiography. *Teaching and Teacher Education*, **128**, 1–10. https://doi.org/10.1016/j.tate.2023.104119.

Singh, N., Getenet, S., & Tualaulelei, E. (2023). Examining students' behavioural engagement in lecture videos with and without embedded quizzes in an online course: People, partnerships and pedagogies. In T. Cochrane, V. Narayan, C. Brown et al. (Eds.), *People, partnerships and pedagogies. Proceedings ASCILITE 2023*. Christchurch: Australasian Society for Computers in Learning in Tertiary Education, pp. 224–233. https://doi.org/10.14742/apubs.2023.571.

Stone, C., Freeman, E., Dyment, J. E., Muir, T., & Milthorpe, N. (2019). Equal or equitable? The role of flexibility within online education. *Australian & International Journal of Rural Education*, **29**(2), 26–40. https://journal.spera.asn.au/index.php/AIJRE/article/view/221.

Stone, C. M. M., & O'Shea, S. E. (2019). My children ... think it's cool that Mum is a uni student: Women with caring responsibilities studying online. *Australasian Journal of Educational Technology*, **35**(6), 97–110. https://doi.org/10.14742/ajet.5504.

Stone, C., O'Shea, S., May, J., Delahunty, J., & Partington, Z. (2016). Opportunity through online learning: Experiences of first-in-family students in online open-entry higher education. *Australian Journal of Adult Learning*, **56**(2), 146–169. https://ajal.net.au/opportunity-through-online-learning-experiences-of-first-in-family-students-in-online-open-entry-higher-education/.

Sugden, N., Brunton, R., MacDonald, J., Yeo, M., & Hicks, B. (2021). Evaluating student engagement and deep learning in interactive online psychology learning activities. *Australasian Journal of Educational Technology*, **37**(2), 45–65. https://doi.org/10.14742/ajet.6632.

Sun, J. C.-Y., Kuo, C. Y., Hou, H. T., & Lin, Y. Y. (2017). Exploring learners' sequential behavioral patterns, flow experience, and learning performance in an anti-phishing educational game. *Educational Technology & Society*, **20**(1), 45–60. www.j-ets.net/collection/published-issues/20_1.

Sung, H.-Y., Hwang, G.-J., Wu, P.-H., & Lin, D.-Q. (2018). Facilitating deep-strategy behaviors and positive learning performances in science inquiry activities with a 3D experiential gaming approach. *Interactive Learning Environments*, **26**(8), 1053–1073. https://doi.org/10.1080/10494820.2018.1437049.

Suwantarathip, O., & Wichadee, S. (2014). The effects of collaborative writing activity using Google docs on students' writing abilities. *Turkish Online Journal of Educational Technology-TOJET*, **13**(2), 148–156. www.tojet.net/articles/v13i2/13215.pdf.

Taşkın, N., & Kılıç Çakmak, E. (2022). Effects of gamification on behavioral and cognitive engagement of students in the online learning environment. *International Journal of Human–Computer Interaction*, **39**(17), 3334–3345. https://doi.org/10.1080/10447318.2022.2096190.

Taylor, J. C. (2001). Fifth generation distance education. *Instructional Science and Technology*, **4**(1), 1–14. https://ascilite.org/archived-journals/e-jist/docs/vol4no1/Taylor.pdf.

Tran, C. J. K., & Lamar, M. F. (2020). Fostering small group discussion in an online instrumental analysis course using Google Docs. *The Journal of Forensic Science Education*, **2**(2), 1–15. https://jfse-ojs-tamu.tdl.org/jfse/article/view/34.

Tualaulelei, E. (2020). The benefits of creating open educational resources as assessment in an online education course. In S. Gregory, S. Warburton, & M. Parkes (Eds.), *ASCILITE's First Virtual Conference. Proceedings ASCILITE 2020*. Armidale: Australasian Society for Computers in Learning in Tertiary Education, pp. 282–288. https://doi.org/10.14742/ascilite2020.0109.

Tualaulelei, E., Burke, K., Fanshawe, M., & Cameron, C. (2021). Mapping pedagogical touchpoints: Exploring online student engagement and course design. *Active Learning in Higher Education*, 23(3), 189–203. https://doi.org/10.1177/1469787421990847.

Van der Meijden, H. (2005). *Knowledge construction through CSCL: Student elaborations in synchronous, asynchronous and 3-D learning environments*. PhD, Radboud Universiteit Nijmegen.

Vytasek, J. M., Patzak, A., & Winne, P. H. (2020). Analytics for student engagement. In *Machine learning paradigms: Advances in learning analytics* (pp. 23–48). Cham: Springer International Publishing.

Wang, F. H. (2019). On the relationships between behaviors and achievement in technology-mediated flipped classrooms: A two-phase online behavioral PLS-SEM model. *Computers & Education*, **142**, 103653. https://doi.org/10.1016/j.compedu.2019.103653.

Wang, Y., & Stein, D. (2021). Effects of online teaching presence on students' cognitive conflict and engagement. *Distance Education*, **42**(4), 547–566. https://doi.org/10.1080/01587919.2021.1987837.

Waters, J., & Gasson, S. (2006). Social engagement in an online community of inquiry: Human-Computer Interaction. In *Proceedings of the Twenty Seventh International Conference on Information Systems*, pp. 1–22. https://cci.drexel.edu/faculty/sgasson/Pubs/JW-SG-ICIS-HCI-03[Final].pdf.

Watty, K., McKay, J., & Ngo, L. (2016). Innovators or inhibitors? Accounting faculty resistance to new educational technologies in higher education. *Journal of Accounting Education*, **36**, 1–15. https://doi.org/10.1016/j.jaccedu.2016.03.003.

Wood, J. (2022). *These 3 charts show the global growth in online learning.* World Economic Forum. www.weforum.org/agenda/2022/01/online-learning-courses-reskill-skills-gap/.

Zee, M., & Koomen, H. M. (2016). Teacher self-efficacy and its effects on classroom processes, student academic adjustment, and teacher well-being: A synthesis of 40 years of research. *Review of Educational Research*, **86**(4), 981–1015. https://doi.org/10.3102/0034654315626801.

Zheng, L. (2015). A systematic literature review of design-based research from 2004 to 2013. *Journal of Computers in Education*, **2**(4), 399–420. https://doi.org/10.1007/s40692-015-0036-z.

Zhu, E. (2006). Interaction and cognitive engagement: An analysis of four asynchronous online discussions. *Instructional Science*, **34**(6), 451–480. https://doi.org/10.1007/s11251-006-0004-0.

Zygouris-Coe, V. I. (2019). Benefits and challenges of collaborative learning in online teacher education. In T. L. Heafner, R. Hartshorne, & R. Thripp (Eds.), *Handbook of research on emerging practices and methods for K-12 online and blended learning*. Hershey, PA: IGI Global, pp. 33–56.

Cambridge Elements

Critical Issues in Teacher Education

Tony Loughland
University of New South Wales

Tony Loughland is an Associate Professor in the School of Education at the University of New South Wales, Australia. Tony is currently leading projects on using AI for citizens' informed participation in urban development, the provision of staffing for rural and remote areas in NSW and on Graduate Ready Schools.

Andy Gao
University of New South Wales

Andy Gao is a Professor in the School of Education at the University of New South Wales, Australia. He edits various internationally-renowned journals, such as International Review of Applied Linguistics in Language Teaching for De Gruyter and Asia Pacific Education Researcher for Springer.

Hoa T. M. Nguyen
University of New South Wales

Hoa T. M. Nguyen is an Associate Professor in the School of Education at the University of New South Wales, Australia. She specializes in teacher education/development, mentoring and sociocultural theory.

Editorial Board

Megan Blumenreich, *CUNY*
Ricardo Cuenca, *Universidad Nacional Mayor de San Marcos, Peru*
Viv Ellis, *Monash University*
Declan Fahie, *UCD Dublin*
Amanda Gutierrez, *ACU Australia*
Jo Lampert, *Monash University*
Lily Orland-Barak, *University of Haifa*
Auli Toom, *University of Helsinki*
Simone White, *RMIT Australia*
Juhan Ye, *BNU China*
Hongbiao Yin, *Chinese University of Hong Kong*
Zhu Xhudong, *BNU China*

About the Series

This series addresses the critical issues teacher educators and teachers are engaged with in the increasingly complex profession of teaching. These issues reside in teachers' response to broader social, cultural and political shifts and the need for teachers' professional education to equip them to teach culturally and linguistically diverse students.

Cambridge Elements⩵

Critical Issues in Teacher Education

Elements in the Series

Interculturality, Criticality and Reflexivity in Teacher Education
Fred Dervin

Enhancing Educators' Theoretical and Practical Understandings of Critical Literacy
Vera Sotirovska and Margaret Vaughn

Reclaiming the Cultural Politics of Teaching and Learning: Schooled in Punk
Greg Vass

Language Teacher's Social Cognition
Hao Xu

Who am I as a Teacher? Migrant Teachers' Redefined Professional Identity
Annika Käck

Professional Supervision for Principals: A Primer for Emerging Practice
Mary Ann Hunter and Geoff Broughton

Decolonizing Pedagogy in Post-Apartheid South Africa: A Post-Vygotskian Ethicopolitical and Ontoepistemic Postulation
Azwihangwisi Edward Muthivhi

Online Teacher Education and Interactive Technologies
Seyum Getenet and Eseta Tualaulelei

A full series listing is available at: www.cambridge.org/EITE

For EU product safety concerns, contact us at Calle de José Abascal, 56–1°, 28003 Madrid, Spain or eugpsr@cambridge.org.

www.ingramcontent.com/pod-product-compliance
Ingram Content Group UK Ltd.
Pitfield, Milton Keynes, MK11 3LW, UK
UKHW022101100226
467896UK00020B/454